TO MARC

ONWARDS AND UPWARDS,
TO GREAT ACHIEVEMENTS
SUCCESS, HAPPINESS AND
TO PURPOSE FELT WITHIN!

The Guiding Purpose Strategy

A Navigational Code for Growth
#Brands #Businesses #People

EXTENDED EDITION

Markus Kramer
with Tofig Husein-zadeh

London | New York

Published by Clink Street Publishing 2020

Copyright © 2020

First published in 2017

Second Edition.

ISBN:
978-1-912262-37-3 hardback
978-1-912262-38-0 paperback
978-1-912262-50-2 ebook

Acknowledgements

My deepest thanks to all of you who contributed through sharp, insightful and forward-looking thinking. I am most grateful for the countless encounters both personally and professionally with so many great brand builders, leaders and people without whom the accumulated experience that led to *The Guiding Purpose Strategy* could never have been achieved. You are generous and kind, in all corners of the world. In this extended edition, many of you have given their time, energy and experience contributing to an even richer perspective of how Purpose propels growth and connects us all. Reto, Sionade, Ivan, Byron, Graeme, Jean-Francois, Dimitrios, Julie, Lilian and Willi: you are not just acclaimed experts in your fields, but generously giving forward – it is much appreciated. A warm thank you also to my co-author Tofig Husein-zadeh for his focus, wisdom and dedication to help me write this navigational map for which no blueprint existed until our kickoff on a mountain top in 2015 and then again in early 2019 for this extended volume. Thank you, Angela M. Harp and Nicole Laine for keeping me on my toes by challenging the thinking and honing the structure and language aspects of this work. And thank you to my editors, Gareth Howard and Hayley Radford for your expert advice and support in getting this edition to the finish line on time once more. But most of all, thank you to my beloved family. Claudia, Isabela, Rafael and Sofia, you are the source of my energy and my passion for life.

Markus Kramer
Summer 2020

Dedicated to those who get that
it's never just business.

"Profit for a company is like oxygen for a person. If you don't have enough of it, you're out of the game. But if you think your life is about breathing, you're really missing something…"

Prof. Peter Ferdinand Drucker
Austrian-born American
Author, Consultant and
Father of Modern Management
(1909–2005)

A note on the Coat of Arms

The North Star on the upper left-hand corner of the shield symbolizes the importance of guidance and progress on one's life journey. It carries archetypal power and a deep meaning that transcends culture, ethnicity, religion and geographical location.

The compass refers to one's current orientation. One who is fully aware of their whereabouts at any given point in time is in a position to map the route, make the necessary decisions and set the path destined for a better place.

The pocket watch reminds us how time forms part of a grand equation and how little time we have to make a real difference. The symbol of the timepiece emphasizes the knowledge that withstands the test of time.

The ship's wheel represents the vital role of becoming a leader and taking control. It stands for self-leadership, the drive to lead in thought, in an organization and in one's own field or market.

In its entirety, the shield protects that which is worth preserving. It gives balance to the concentrated power of each of the key symbols with which it has been mindfully adorned. If the symbols collectively communicate positive progress, the shield then communicates protection and preservation – all is connected, operating as one.

A Word On The Extended Edition

If anything, the past five years were a validation of the soundness not just of Purpose as transformative force, but of the thoroughness of the principles and frameworks described in this book. Hence, we would like to thank everyone who has read the first edition of *The Guiding Purpose Strategy, A Navigational Code for Brand Growth* as well as the many professionals out there who are actively using the *Guiding Purpose Strategy Framework* in their daily work to help guide clients, businesses, brands and people towards successful futures. And we extend of course a very warm welcome to anyone who comes across this book for the first time.

It is important to iterate that *GPS* was never intended to be a 101-business book and if anything, this extended edition is an amplification of this: it has been enriched and broadened in numerous dimensions. New chapters and contributions from thought-leaders across cultures, spheres of business, academia and practitioners alike help to demonstrate just how important clarity of Purpose is in our times and how transformational its effects can be. In our humble view, the inclusion of key contributors adds a richness and depth of perspectives that we hope will be enlightening and inspirational to you.

This extended edition of *GPS* explores the relationship between Purpose and growth more closely on a cultural and economic level. Purpose and profit for instance are no opposites. Rather, the continued convergence of the two can help companies build long-term growth and sustainable ways to create competitive advantage. We put our view forward that the world needs to see more industries and organizations genuinely adopt Purpose-driven leadership as part of their long-term thinking. It is for the good of companies, brands and their people. And whilst Purpose transformation needs to remain first and foremost an economic model for companies to build their future on, it is also an indispensable way of thinking, contributing to the well-being of our planet and the generations to come.

We invite you to see this *extended* edition of the *GPS* in the way the Canadian media effects analyst Dr Marshall McLuhan saw extensions of media. Language does for intelligence what the wheel does for the feet. In other words, language extends intelligence: "A good reader, a highly literate person, tends to be a good executive." A book, as he correctly discovered, is an extension of the eye.

Enjoy this extended edition of *The Guiding Purpose Strategy*!

Contents

Initiation

Welcome

"Truth is the beginning of every good to the gods,
and of every good to man."

Plato
Father of Western Philosophy

The very fact that you are reading these lines may indicate that you are one of the select few intent on making change happen. We cannot define your reasoning, but we can confidently say that we will provide you with an *all-Purpose tool* to master your journey towards change. Think of it as a Swiss Army Knife of some sort – beautiful, simple, effective and easy to use. Once you learn how to use it, you will find it convenient to carry with you wherever you go. But beware: it is not a toy and it will require a little time and patience to learn how to craft with it.

We believe that the coming era will be one of radical transparency. For businesses, brands and their leaders, the implications are powerful, albeit not exactly obvious. So, what is it going to take to create thriving value propositions, products, and services, and indeed to anchor ourselves in this new post-positioning period of total connectedness?

As societies mature, economic development accelerates, and competitive pressure continues to increase, our individual and collective craving for orientation is on the rise. A statistical analysis of text content over the last two centuries supports this notion. Google Books Ngram Viewer analyzes the vast content of millions of books and outputs a graph that represents and contrasts the use of a particular term throughout time.

Google Ngram on Leadership and Strategy

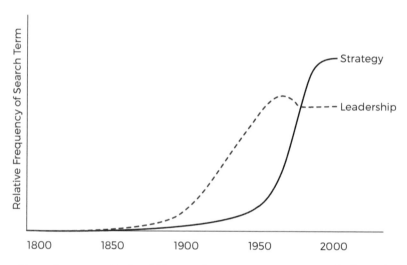

Note the steep climb of 'Strategy' entering into our vocabulary. Strategy intertwined with leadership takes us to a desired future. For example, achieving a personal objective or reaching targets in business. However, we claim that neither will be enough to master the future successfully. We see Purpose as the North Star providing guidance and direction. We are not suggesting that Leadership or Strategy will become less important, but rather that these critical areas will need to be boosted by adding meaning to whatever you do in order to become or stay successful in the future.

A meaningful brand driven by a higher Purpose drives profits. Purposeful brands outperform the stock market by 133%; gain 46% more share of wallet and achieve marketing results that are double those of lower rated brands.[1] But real Purpose goes beyond profit and certainly beyond 'Corporate Social Responsibility' and all the fancy reports that brush over the underlying, often systemic issues. Business models properly centered on Purpose build beneficial relationships with external stakeholders and drive culture from within. A sense of real Purpose has numerous positive effects. Perhaps most importantly, it has a major impact on job satisfaction.[2]

The Guiding Purpose Strategy is in many ways a reflection of our society. In writing this book, it was certainly invaluable to put it up against a new industrial context where the convergence of attitudes and consumption behavior among younger generations can be seen through a different lens. *The Guiding Purpose Strategy* – in short *GPS* – is an instrument to discover Purpose, the main ingredient needed to create and sustain a meaningful brand, a business or indeed a life. It provides a transferable methodology that promises to increase returns and improve results, both literally and intrinsically.

Building on many years of experience in working with some of the most inspiring brands in the world, from consumer products, to government institutions, to charities and tech startups, we demonstrate how the application of the *GPS Framework* can help create value systems that lead to prosperity at both an organizational and an individual level. We pay particular attention to the luxury sector, an industry in which passion and Purpose-driven brands have stood the test of time.

For the underpinning explorations of this book to be fruitful, we thought it best to remain open to serendipitous possibilities. One never knows from whom or from where the next big thing might come. So instead of limiting ourselves to the 'business' or 'social science' shelves, we also looked in unexpected places. We spoke with younger and older generations, leaders, entrepreneurs, brand experts and many others. Our research had to go beyond the heap of traditional management material. It also had to be multilingual, taking into account large amounts of data not yet translated into English. As authors from different cultural backgrounds and generations, we took advantage of the opportunity to combine our worlds of Eastern wisdom and Western constructivism. To enrich our minds even further, we referenced various works of enlightenment, drawing knowledge from a range of sources, including Greek philosophers to more recent marketing case studies, academic lectures and scholarly articles.

As we believe intellectuals have done enough dividing and too little assembling, we are intent on taking an interdisciplinary approach. That is to say, we follow the old alchemical maxim *solve et coagula*, which means to dissolve and coagulate, analyze and synthesize. Our interdisciplinary take on Purpose involves examining across and in between fields, cultures, relationships, etc. As Rory Sutherland, Vice-Chairman of Ogilvy Group UK, so eloquently put it "the most interesting thing that's happening in any field is not in any field, it's actually in the interplay between different fields."

It is the individuals and companies with clarity of Purpose that are changing the world, bit by bit. Leaders, marketers, entrepreneurs and professionals who understand the power of inner Purpose are destined to become the positive changemakers of tomorrow. In the words of Paul Polman, ex-CEO of Unilever, "Business does not exist to make a profit. It makes a profit to exist. We must not forget our Purpose."

Our intention is to pass on the *spirit and mindset* with which *The Guiding Purpose Strategy* book was written. So, if you are looking for a typical step-by-step strategy book, you might be better-off looking elsewhere. If you're up for a journey towards professional and personal growth – we are excited to have you on board!

Eliminating Low Definitions

"Analgesics that are branded are more effective at reducing pain
than analgesics that are not branded.
I don't just mean through reported pain reduction,
but actual measured pain reduction."

Rory Sutherland
Perspective is Everything
TED conference

A concept central to this book is the notion of brand, or in other words, the image you portray onto others. Regardless of whether you are reading this for business or personal growth – or both. Essentially, brand value is the ultimate currency companies, and increasingly more individuals, crave. Sir John Hegarty, co-founder of BBH and one of the world's most awarded ad men said it best: "Don't start a business, build a brand."[3]

However, as long as we keep describing the notion of 'a brand' in a confusing way, we will continue to have a vague understanding of it. So, let's start by defining what a brand is. A brand differentiates something or someone from its competition and instills trust, simplifies choice by reducing risk, spurs demand and creates pricing power and – all being well – builds loyalty and creates value over time. At the time of writing, the most valuable brand in the world is Apple, with a whopping US$234 billion in brand worth.[4] Clearly, when things are done right, brands manage to create tremendous amounts of economic value. We can derive from this that 'brand' is something hugely valuable, yet miraculously intangible.

You might not become the next Apple, but there is still a lot to learn from the concept of brand. In early Egypt, Rome and Greece, for instance, merchants painted their storefronts and hung pictorial signs to communicate what goods they had on offer to a mostly illiterate population. Historically, branding mostly meant stamping things. In other words, this was about claiming objects by putting your name or your mark on it. Cowboys would brand their cows, hence our modern term 'brand' or 'branding', which derives from the iron rod used to 'brand' an animal. This helped cattlemen collect their livestock at the end of the day from the vast prairies. It also made it easier for them to sell their cattle. A good 'brand' on an animal could be trusted. And trust equals money. So, let's hold the thought that *Branding endows products and services with the power of the brand.*

In medieval times and later during the Renaissance and the Enlightenment, prominent architects and stonemasons would leave symbols on the monumental cathedrals and palaces they built in the hope of being recognized by other guild members for their efforts.

Today, branding is still about leaving a mark. But as competitive pressure increases, so too does the effort of marketers to stand out – and sell more. The consequence? Brands are all too often promising more than they can deliver. However, whilst overpromising offers short term fixes, it runs counterintuitive to building a strong brand. Real brand trust is earned, not bought – and consumers know this. Havas Media's study captioned 'Meaningful Brands' shows that consumers wouldn't even care, let alone feel the difference if almost 70% of existing brands disappeared from the face of the earth.[5]

It is also easy to assume that 'being a brand' equates to simply being a big company – like Apple. But remember, even Apple started humbly. Cameron Craig, a communications professional, who did PR for Apple for ten years, learned from his journey that brand is a valuable asset: "Most importantly, respect your brand. That's the biggest lesson of all that I learned at Apple. It's your biggest asset and you have to protect it." Indeed, people come and go. Brands, if managed carefully over time, remain top of mind with consumers far longer than employees stay with a company.

As we progress on our journey towards finding, articulating and harnessing the idea of a strongly rooted Purpose that can deliver integrity inside and out, we must learn about the intricacies of differentiating, positioning, creating unique value propositions and building a loyal audience through the power of brand. But where should we look? Firstly, anyone navigating towards a substantially better future requires a map to get there.

From Cartography to GPS

*"The real voyage of discovery consists not
in seeking new landscapes but in having new eyes."*

Marcel Proust
French Novelist

Map-making has taken us from navigating land and sea, to mapping history, understanding business processes and even decoding our own origins. It seems only natural that the concept of the North Star can serve us well in outlining a *Guiding Purpose Strategy*.

Regardless of whether you're a firm, a brand, or an individual, you will need to implement specific strategies on how to grow, to thrive and to achieve permanent success. The science and art of such stratagem is based on orientation. In order to thrive, you first need to know exactly where you are. This means being totally honest with yourself about where you currently stand and how solid your stance is. It is of course equally important to understand where you want to end up – ideally, even down to the exact address of your final destination. The instrument that allows you to pinpoint a desired destination is also the instrument that will take you there.

Understanding the role of maps and having a good sense of direction has always been essential for leaders and entrepreneurs across industries and throughout history in order to conquer and win in their fields. Let's take a moment and travel back in time to refresh our memories on the history of mankind's relationship with cartography.

Merriam Webster's Dictionary[6] defines cartography as:

1. The process or skill to draw maps
2. The science or art of making maps

It is worth noting that the earliest known maps were of the heavens, not of the earth. The earliest cartographers were also the first experts in geometry and astronomy. As masters of calculation, they were called on to consult the kings and pharaohs in ancient times.

Buckminster Fuller, the futurologist who was awarded the Royal Gold Medal for Architecture, writes about a successful group of mapmakers and explorers in his book, *The World Men*. Fuller describes them as being extraordinary at designing vessels and carrying out expeditions in a strategic manner: "They had high proficiency in dealing with celestial navigation, the storms, the sea, the men, the ship, economics, biology, geography, history, and science. The wider and longer-more distanced their anticipatory strategy, the more successful they became." These World Men were especially triumphant during the Age of Exploration, also known as the Age of Discovery. They were the great adventurers, mapmakers and seafarers of the times. Through their processes of experimentation, measuring and inventing, they inevitably developed fortune-producing enterprises.

It is due to the adventurous spirit of history's brave explorers that the North Star became the functional anchor for orientation. World explorers, excursionists, travelers and voyagers passed through boundless deserts guided by its light. The North Star hence marks a constant and reliable source of orientation in an ever-changing, unpredictable world.

In the time of Ferdinand and Isabella of Spain, as well as other maritime monarchs, maps were kept top-secret.[7] At the time, map-making was not just about mapping geographic territory or destination points. Some began mapping in other fields like architecture and biology, too. The wayfarers, the architect- and sculptor-guilds who planted the first seeds of the Renaissance were also aware of the beneficial functions of map-making. Likewise, botanists and zoologists saw the value of mapping plants and animals. Mapping the human anatomy, however, remained taboo for quite some time. In fact, it was prohibited up until 1315 when Mondino de Luzzi, an Italian surgeon, published *Anatomia*, the first manual and map on dissection.

Map-making was also an integral part of firms, although not commonly known outside the business world. Merchants and entrepreneurs often took advantage of travelers with business acumen for their cartographic skills in trading processes or building an enterprise. Maps helped increase efficiency, as decisions could be made based on measurement and analysis, while operations could be simplified, and workflows documented. Cartography was instrumental in turning management into a science, as business process mapping started to demystify the complexities of an organization. A business process map allows for alignment on what route is best taken in order to make improvements to a particular process, perhaps increasing efficiency, delivering a product quicker or making customer experience better.

Nonetheless, the idea of business maps – namely, detailed diagrams of a company's operations and workflows – did not reach their heights until the beginning of the 20th century. For example, Allan H. Mogensen, an American industrial engineer and authority in the field of work simplification, began training business people in the 1930s in map-making. One of his students, Art Spinanger used his newly acquired business map-making skills to help Procter & Gamble streamline its operations.

With the invention of electric and digital technologies came the revolution of cartography. Maps could now be regularly and instantly updated, which greatly improved their accuracy. Towards the end of the 20th century humanity found ways to create a genetic map. The completion of genome mapping will certainly be a critical turning point, not just in the history of cartography. "Like the system of interstate highways spanning our country, the map of the human genome will be completed stretch by stretch," says James Watson, the Nobel Prize Laureate and co-discoverer of the structure of DNA.[8]

We've definitely come a long way since de Luzzi's original maps of the human anatomy. Cartography of the body has evolved to a point where scientists have constructed a map of the brain and can identify which parts of the brain react to specific images, sounds or situations, thanks to technologies such as electroencephalography (EEG) or functional magnetic resonance imaging (fMRI). These types of development made way for today's prospering field of neuromarketing. Marketers began measuring various product-related characteristics, such as the crunchy sounds of potato chip packaging, in order to identify what types of tonality ignites signals of arousal in the brain of the consumer when touching the packaged good. Most neuromarketing experts agree on the fact that the importance of visual storytelling in brand communications cannot be overstated. Indeed, storytelling began with the shamans of ancient cultures. And neuroscience has shown that the ancient skill of storytelling and creating narratives of legends and myths is a pastime that is not only still very much alive – it prevails.

May Britt-Moser and Edvard I. Moser were awarded the 2014 Nobel Prize for their discovery of cells that constitute a positioning system in the brain. They claimed to have discovered "an 'inner GPS' in the brain that makes it possible to orient ourselves in space, demonstrating a cellular basis for higher cognitive function."[9] Thanks to our inner GPS, we know where we are, and we know how we are able to find our way from one place to another. Essentially, we store information in such a way that we can immediately trace our steps the next time we take the same path.

If we were to travel back a century, we would see that secret intelligence service agencies had the first Global Positioning System. Its invention changed everything, operating in real time, which saved huge amounts of time in reaching target points during investigations. For a long time, a GPS was just an idea explored in Hollywood movies. Today, if you have a smartphone in your pocket, a GPS is always with you.

The Global Positioning System is an indication of how we have successfully mapped the *outer* world – its nautical and aeronautical maps help us orientate and navigate our way around. However, we are still missing a key, kind of a navigational instrument, to guide us inwardly. If companies, leaders, brands and entrepreneurs are to secure their future, they must create a map of their *inner* worlds. According to research from Jonathan Trevor, Associate Professor of Management Practice at Saïd Business School, University of Oxford, the key to creating and sustaining a winning organization is to ensure the company is strategically aligned – arranging all elements of an organization to optimally support the fulfillment of its long-term Purpose.[10]

We live in times of unprecedented change, which requires us to connect and think beyond the parameters of the GPS we know today. It is time to take what we have inherited from a long history of cartographers a step further and create a map that leads us to our inner North Star. Just think of it as a new dimension of the GPS, one that points us in the direction of what makes us thrive.

However, not all is known – and hence we continue to explore the world as we know it, thereby continuing to expand our own understanding and the world, or indeed the universe, we live in.

If you have come this far, you have just discovered our rationale for calling this new inner, guiding instrument *The Guiding Purpose Strategy*, a.k.a. GPS.

Purposeful Pursuit of The Unknown

"When seen from space, national boundaries are invisible and conflicts dividing people imperceptible."

Dr Sionade Robinson
Contributing Author, Associate Dean, People & Culture,
Cass Business School, London

I grew up watching Gene Roddenberry's *Star Trek*. From the moment Captain Kirk solemnly intoned the Purpose of space exploration, I was captivated: *"Space: the final frontier. These are the voyages of the Starship Enterprise. Its five-year mission: to explore strange new worlds. To seek out new life and new civilizations. To boldly go where no man has gone before."*

Little did I know Captain James T. Kirk's quest was a copycat space age homage to eighteenth century British navigator, explorer and cartographer Captain James Cook, whose five year mission, on the voyages of the naval ship Endeavour, was to discover new lands and go not only *"farther than any other man has been before me, but as far as I think it possible for man to go."*

Of course, humankind's interest in *"going beyond"* began much earlier than Captain Cook. Since our ancestors made their way from Africa 50,000 or 60,000 years ago, Homo Sapiens' urge to scale mountains, cross oceans, endure extreme conditions and now perhaps to leave our planet for another is arguably a differentiating characteristic of our species. Around the world in every modern and ancient culture, in legends, oral traditions, art, humanities and science, those who undertake such feats – we call them explorers – are celebrated and admired.

Why? Perhaps a clue lies in the definition of exploration itself. It is distinct from nomadic wandering, pilgrimage or a diplomatic or trading mission. While exploration may be motivated by many things – a quest for resources, imperial advantage, commerce or an expansionist belief system – it is essentially an exercise in the creation of new and valuable knowledge, collected under special conditions. These special conditions are illustrated in the ambitions of both Cook and Kirk – *exploration creates new knowledge (and value) through the conscious and purposeful pursuit of the unknown.* Exploration may lead to discovery, but discovery is only the beginning, Explorers create paths for others to follow. Let's look at how this happens by unpacking this definition of exploration as *a conscious and purposeful pursuit of the unknown* a little further.

Firstly, the *conscious* dimension of exploration prompts explorers to become storytellers. Journals, books, public lectures have long been part of an explorer's role in knowledge creation and their accounts often reveal the prevailing attitudes of their times. Pursuing the unknown means crossing a boundary between what we already think and believe and other possibilities. It might also cause us to question why such a boundary exists in the first place. For example, in the late 1950s, when NASA was new, the list of spaceflight unknowns was long. One concern was how potential astronauts would endure the anticipated motion sickness of space flight. To begin their research, NASA enrolled 11 deaf men whose condition meant they were immune to motion sickness. All but one were deaf after childhood spinal meningitis, which can cause lasting damage to the vestibular system of the inner ear by the killing nerve and hair cells vital to giving our brains information about motion, balance, and even spatial orientation. In space, this system stops receiving the gravitational cues that distinguish up and down, but one's eyes still see things normally generating conflicting information leading to a space sickness much like seasickness. The men who became known as the Gallaudet Eleven took part in experiments to calibrate the machines that would train astronauts for spaceflight. One test involved four men inside a 20-foot slow rotation room that spun at ten revolutions per minute for 12 consecutive days. Another involved zero-g flights in the so-called "Vomit Comet" so that scientists could look for stress hormones in their urine. Of course, there was no question any of the Gallaudet Eleven would ever serve as astronauts themselves. They were excluded from even applying *because they were deaf.* A boundary NASA is yet to go beyond.

Secondly *the Purpose of pursuit* prompts many interesting discussions in the context of space exploration. How is aspiring to become an interplanetary species justifiable, when there is plenty of work to do here at home? For the fifty years or more humans have explored space there is a well-rehearsed argument that it has generated a continuing flow of societal benefits, though these are surely merely serendipitous. During the 1960s, unmanned spacecraft photographed and probed the moon before astronauts ever landed. By the early 1970s, orbiting communications and navigation satellites were in everyday use and the Mariner spacecraft was already mapping the surface of Mars. In the 1980s, satellite communications expanded to carry television programs, discovered an ozone hole over Antarctica, pinpointed forest fires and gave us photographs of the nuclear power plant disaster at Chernobyl in 1986. Clearly it wasn't only Velcro and Teflon that we took away. Everyone who has worked, is working and will work in the space industry does so at a higher level of precision and expertise than had existed before space exploration came along.

The question remains: can terrestrial benefit be the real reason we invest in space exploration? It might be the basis of a business case to demonstrate long term return on investment, but the purpose of space exploration isn't just to create the needed technological solutions. . The purpose is to drive society itself forward. The space program is the modern equivalent of *building cathedrals*, a shared enterprise celebrating vision and talent and inspiring awe and wonder. Many societies across many ages have built monuments to their beliefs and did so in such a way as to illustrate the epitome of their shared creative achievement. Few of us can stand in such places and not feel the ambitions, commitment and values of the societies who made them. Some argue Space exploration is our *cathedral to the unknown*, our monuments to the future, inspiring awe, wonder and curiosity in equal measure.

The way space exploration creates this unifying sense of awe is illustrated in the reports of the 'Overview Effect' experienced by many astronauts from both the Apollo missions and the International Space Station. The Overview Effect is the cognitive shift in awareness during spaceflight when viewing the Earth from outer space. It is the story told by many of these extraordinary explorers of what it feels like to witness the reality of the Earth in space, national boundaries invisible and conflicts dividing people imperceptible. Michael Collins, Apollo 11 put it as follows "*The thing that really surprised me was that it [Earth] projected an air of fragility. And why, I don't know. I don't know to this day. I had a feeling it's tiny, it's shiny, it's beautiful, it's home, and it's fragile.*"[11]

Wishing to mobilize this powerful effect, Space For Humanity (S4H) is a non-profit headquartered in Denver, Colorado with the goal of sending 10,000 diverse humans to the edge of space, low earth orbit, the moon, and deep space to democratize space and create ambassadors for earth bound programs to deliver the United Nations Sustainable Goals and improve the state of the world.

At present there are many commercial, as well as governmental, space agencies actively developing plans and technologies for the exploration of space. Critics of these plans, quite rightly, point to the need to invest in saving our home planet first, taking action on climate change, rising sea levels, pollution and ocean acidification. After all, we only have a decade to save the Earth.

So, what if the real Purpose of space exploration is much more than just return on monetary investment. Societies are doomed in the long run if they place their resources and their efforts into enterprises that don't deliver concrete value but the missions of businesses currently investing seem to stretch further. Blue Origin seeks to "build a road to space for our children." Planetary Resources seeks to "identify and unlock the critical water resources necessary for human expansion in space." And SpaceX seeks to "revolutionize space technology with the ultimate goal of enabling people to live on other planets." These indeed illustrate the conscious and Purposeful pursuit of the unknown.

We must discuss Purpose openly. Space exploration, like its earthbound predecessor, is a shared enterprise, requiring partnerships and collaboration around a common goal and creates new opportunities to tell powerful stories about values. Space exploration contributes to trust and diplomacy between nations and it may be that it is only through collaboration in space we shall find a way to take care of Spaceship Earth. Buckminster Fuller put it precisely: *"We are not going to be able to operate our Spaceship Earth successfully nor for much longer unless we see it as a whole spaceship and our fate as common. It has to be everybody or nobody."*

Exploring Growth

*"The most exciting breakthroughs of the 21st century
will not occur because of technology,
but because of an expanded concept of what it means to be human."*

John Naisbitt
Futurist and Author

Is growth good? To answer this question, we need to examine the role of 'growth' from multiple angles. A good starting point is anthropology (from *anthropos* – human), the science that studies human beings empirically, as it is often referred to as the most scientific of humanities and the most humane of sciences.

As a process, 'growth' is of high value not only for progressivist societies around the world but even for the smallest of tribes outside of modern or urban cultures. Growth as a concept is of such high significance that many societies mark it with ceremonies. From birth to childhood to becoming an adult, being initiated to a hidden circle or knowledge, getting married or elevating in social status – all are celebrated with traditional rituals and symbolism worldwide. Despite the differences among ethnicities and cultures, valuing growth is a common denominator. Constructivist in its essence, growth is an upright process filled with notable milestones, which are seen as its results and rewards. The example of tribes with their own identities, rituals, symbols and artistic traditions also shows that a meaning system can grow without an economic system in place, but no economic system can grow without a meaning or value system as its underpinning.

Hence, growth can take on many different forms. There is exponential growth that can be explained by Moore's Law. Growth can be financial, cultural, physical, internal or all together. Then there is stable growth, organic growth, holistic growth, mathematical and geometrical growth. There are also new, creative cost-effective and exploratory ways linked to growth. Growth-hacking, for example, is experimental as it involves thinking while doing rather than thinking ahead of doing. Whilst it might offer an interesting approach to achieve growth for some, for others it will be a step too far outside their comfort zone. Either way, growth stops when one loses the orientation between where he or she stands and where one could or would like to be.

It would also be too easy to associate growth with change, since change is not always growth just as movement is not always progress. Growth for the sake of growth isn't fulfilling because not all growth is healthy. Whilst many have benefited from economic growth during industrialization or more recently through globalization, plenty of people have lost out along the way and are poorer off then 'pre-growth' of economies, for instance.

So, we need to adopt a rather more selective perspective on how we see, plan and think about growth more holistically. Jim Heskett wrote that "growth in a chain of enablers, such as education, has the potential for leading directly to the development of ideas that actually expand the limits of even those kinds of growth that rely on physical resources with supposedly finite properties."[12] According to Angelo Giovas "the key is not more outward growth (which has limits) but more inward renewal (no limits)." It must not be growth for the sake of growth but the betterment of humanity. Meaning, new ways need to be formulated for a better understanding of the limits of growth while being pro-growth.

An outgrowth of unhealthy growth are poor products and services, and consequently weak brands. Facing competitive and financial pressure results in less time spent on the development of a given effort; whether a product, service, campaign etc. In extremis, it can lead to efficiency fetishism and it inevitably results in low quality output that bring no real or lasting value to the buyer, let alone to society.

In our humble view there is no such thing as healthy and humanized growth without a greater Purpose radiating from within. A cultural anchor that channels both energy and integrity. Healthy growth is good when it springs from capitalist cultures that transform, evolve and metamorphose into cultured capitalism. This applies to people, businesses and societies at large.

But growth does not just 'happen'. In our context, people drive growth with great intention, whether at a personal or organizational level. As we shall see in the next chapter, transformational growth is an act of will and careful balance

Actioning Transformation Levers

"A 'higher dimension of consciousness' is crucial
in driving successful organizational transformation"

Ivan Schouker
Contributing Author, Managing Partner and
Founder at Finarchitects

Consultancies, business schools and technology firms offer a plethora of Digital Transformation services and intellectual capital platforms that echo the Business Process Reengineering[13] consulting wave of the early 90s and the one accompanying Y2K (Year2000 bug fixing programs). It is a conundrum then that Digital Transformation projects have resulted in large operational risks and over US$900 billion in wasted resources in 2019[14] alone. Yet transformation is not an option.

A study from the BCG Henderson Institute shows that the lifespan of public companies has nearly halved since the 1960s, uncorrelated to type of business or industry. This implies that there is more than a 30% chance that over the next five years a typical tenured CEO and an average investor horizon will see the mortality of his company and investment.

Perhaps the way we have looked at transformation is partly to blame. Rather than conceiving it as a onetime project with onerous internal and external resource mobilization, high expectations and oversold outcomes, transformation ought to be viewed as a habit embedded in the biology of the organization's ecosystem. Firms that have successfully and regularly transformed, going through great upheavals, maintain their distinct DNA. For example, Nokia started in 1865 as a pulp mill before shifting to electricity generation and then mobile phones. At one time, its brand was even used on galoshes; the 'Connecting People' brand also flirted with its 'Kodak moment' in the consumer mobile telephone space. With innovation and service quality strengths translated as 'We create the technology to connect the world', it is today the world's second largest telecoms equipment manufacturer behind Huawei.[15]

What is Purpose-led Transformation? And how can an Inside-Out approach be as powerful on a business level as for personal development?[16] And how can the bellwether that is the Brand, come out strengthened and supportive of growth?

Three decades of transformation practice, from startups to Fortune 500 companies, across sectors and cultural contexts, underscore that successful transformations involve multipronged sustained efforts and cycles of learning and re-equilibrium from within.

These 'higher dimensions of consciousness'[17] are typically to be found within seven levers of organizational transformation. They are like interdependent beehives of value creation that combine to drive business growth. Although one of the dimensions may be a focal point following a diagnosed urgency, it is essential that all of these dimensions are addressed. Imbalance within this beehive is the underpinning cause of lower than expected growth if not of actual failure. Often a mirage, acquisition strategies are relied upon by organizations to provide transformative answers. However, research consistently suggests that 70% of transformational acquisitions or mergers don't meet expectations.[18] The impact of raising consciousness of what can be done with what already exists is underestimated. A simple framework can help guide self-examination and incorporate the habit of transformation into all organizations.

The Purpose Transformation Levers[19]

- *Vision and Values* – The Post-Industrial or Knowledge Age of the 21st Century is full of yearning for identity. Challenges abound from new technologies to belief systems, artificial intelligence to fundamentalism, battering humanity's inherent need for self-determination; and the simple questions of 'who are we' and 'why are we here' or 'what do we stand for' are more salient and complex than ever in the arena of corporate differentiation. In fact, it is in times of upheavals that one can appreciate the value of meaning – hence the rewriting of the past, the development of a new narrative can help in a therapeutic way to reinvent how one looks at its own environment and capabilities. Consumer industry behemoths such as Proctor & Gamble are being deeply disrupted not only because of growing influencer and celebrity social media channels[20] scaling in a low-cost way new pertinent product propositions, but also because of the rise of VC-backed circular economy brands[21]. For example, BlueLand[22] is reinventing household cleaning products with reusable bottles and tablet based eco-friendly detergents; a transformative story for a plastics and harmful chemicals conscious generation.

- **Strategy** – Not long ago, a strategy used to be laid out as a five-year plan. Now corporations work on three-year plans at best. A 'zoom in/zoom out'[23] approach becomes necessary in a world 'that defies prediction'[24] and requires constant focus on learning and agility. Time horizon does not matter as much as depth of thinking on the paths to be taken. When backed by a long-term vision, traditional market boundaries can be more easily challenged and new pathways discovered. A core process here is to examine one's positioning in the value chain mapped against existing and potential capabilities; the digital world compels us to do so because it has lowered barriers to entry in most economic activities. Working on strategies for technology startups and for companies under stress sharpens the mind to optimize chosen avenues under scarce resources. The practice of hard thinking about fundamentals, in a collaborative fashion under time constraints, challenging and validating basic assumptions with rigor could well be emulated by incumbents. Therefore, being agile and constructing multiple advantages are capabilities not strategies. Technology, and digital in particular, should be seen as enablers opening up possibilities, as long as it is coherent with the vision.

- **Technology** – It is important to recast technology to its true role; one that facilitates core processes (data management, communications, client interfaces, etc.) or helps redefine a business model such as platform models which change sources of customer value and costs of delivering it. Digital technologies simplify, reduce and accelerate execution cycles. They allow personalization while entry barriers have lowered for standard offerings. For example, application program interfaces (APIs)[25] design and architecture facilitate communications between software and has opened opportunities for forging alliances and partnerships across industries permitting companies to focus on the proprietary areas of their value chain. In finance, APIs are driving an explosion of innovation and new applications allowing legacy institutions to transform, especially in highly specialized and regulated areas such as risk management.[26] To navigate these IT transformations, insiders as cross-functional teams and closely connected members of the gig economy network, deeply connected to the company's purpose, ought to lead. One-size-fits-all consultants commercializing 'best practices' may bring outside-in guidance and ease the political aspects of change management but, if in the driving seat, pose a danger of introducing short-lived and expensive solutions. Similarly, purely IT-led transformations can over-stretch resources and lose sight of the expected ROI.

- **Economics** – A deep understanding and regular assessment of how the business creates revenues, its capital structure (family, cooperative, listed, etc.) and incentives systems are intimately part of transformation efforts. Subscription models are redefining the economics of software firms; platform and peer-to-peer models revolutionize customer interactions. When matters of sustainability and social responsibility come to the fore, whole new spaces of economic value emerge. The case of Patagonia shows how economic model thinking is at the heart of the success of this well-known social Purpose-driven company[27]. Its quadrupling of profits and revenues, now debt free, over the past ten years led by its former CFO then CEO, Rose Marcario[28], is attributed to the 'Triple Bottom Line' approach: Planet, People, Profits – as will be explained further in the following chapter on 'Purpose & Profit'. The prospect of moving from linear to circular economic models[29] opens a whole new world of value creation.

- **People** – At the heart of a sustainable business is the chemistry of employee talents and of a distinct and diverse culture that brings about powerful collective intelligence. In his best-selling 2004 book, *The Wisdom of Crowds,* James Surowiecki popularized research in part initiated in the early 1900s by Sir Francis Galton[30] which shows that a group of independent thinkers, diverse and empowered individuals, produces better results than individual experts. Transformation 'as a habit' has amongst its imperatives to maintain such environment and ensure teams are optimized. While many lament the challenges of acquiring talent, more cost-effective and smarter opportunities lie in allocating the right talent at the right place at the right time. In *Talent Wins*[31], the authors cite the G3 Transformation leadership team (CEO, CFO, CHRO) brought together by the CEO of Marsh, the giant insurance broker and risk manager. By elevating human capital to the same footing as financial capital, executives initiated successful turnarounds in as diverse businesses as in McGraw-Hill and Tata Communications.

- *Governance* – It is startling to commonly witness how a lack of formal Board processes (executive, non-executive, and/or advisory) can lead to dysfunctional management, block growth and in some instances, destroy value. In particular, the technology and software development worlds abound with smart founders and executives who, despite valuable counsel received from incubators and accelerators, ignore the fundamentals of governance at their expense and risk. Organizational wellness and high-quality governance mechanisms are invisible protective coatings around a Brand's strength; especially in times of crises when the experience of Board members is vital for complex problem-solving and managing reputational risks.

- *Being* – Brand value and health is regularly measured and can be worth billions. It is the visible and tangible expression of the equilibrium across 'dimensions of consciousness.' Harvey Golub, the legendary transformative Chairman and CEO of American Express, engaged over his tenure in several transformation loops that shaped the company into one of the world's most admired firms. His explanation of his approach was simple: make all employees understand what the brand stands for. "If everyone understands that, we won't need thick employee manuals, management training programs, or pricing schedules for the services we sell. Everyone will instinctively do the right thing."[32] On a personal level, he shared "Only after leaving the company will you be aware of and able to appreciate the leadership ethos, capabilities and demands that the American Express brand instill."

Purpose-led Transformations are like musical scores: if you try to focus on the parts, you will sub-optimize the whole or bring dissonance.

In his study of successful and long-lived companies, *The Living Company*,[33] Dutch business theorist Arie De Geus states "companies die because their managers focus on the economic activity of producing goods and services, and they forget that their organizations' true nature is that of a community of human beings that is in business to stay alive."

Today's CEO mission is more than ever to action transformational levers in parallel and in concert. At any time, the chosen equilibrium serves the community by inspiring meaning, clear pathways, appropriate and flexible tools, diversified earning models, optimized talent management and solid steering processes. In a symbiotic manner, he or she embraces brand ambassadorship to promote who the community is and how it fits into the world.

Purpose & Profit

"I think if the people who work for a business are proud of the business they work for, they'll work that much harder, and therefore, I think turning your business into a real force for good is good business sense as well."

Sir Richard Branson
Founder of Virgin Group and British Business Magnate

Most conventional board and executive perspectives still separate profit and Purpose as two diametrical opposites. Whilst vision statements and value systems are crafted, these fall short when faced with economic decisions vs. what would be the right thing to do. The arguments for not linking the two more closely range from good intent but economic fear ("We can't afford to charge our customers more for building more schools in Namibia") to outright ignorance ("We are here to make money, nothing more, nothing less").

Purpose & Profit are still seen as opposites

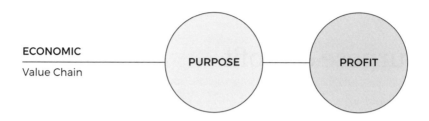

The evidence available to underpin that Purpose and profit can be linked is astounding. Employees are three times more likely to stay at Purpose-driven companies.[34] In addition, the workforce is 1.4 times more engaged and 1.7 times more satisfied at Purpose-driven companies. In times of decreasing relevancy at both individual and organizational levels, disruptive forces are challenging organizations to reassess how value is created and how people (especially younger generations) fit into an evolved worldview. A study by PwC found that millennials who have a strong connection to the Purpose of their organization are 5.3 times more likely to stay.[35] Thus, putting Purpose at the core of a corporation's thinking offers a collective way to close the growing gap between competitive edge and meaningful work.

Business models properly centered on Purpose build beneficial relationships with external stakeholders and drive culture from within. Successful and future-oriented businesses are increasingly seeing Purpose transformation as a powerful differentiator grounded in humanity, building trust, increasing loyalty and inspiring action. Moreover, it is a means for talent attraction and gaining consumer trust. Some 89% of consumers believe Purpose-driven companies will deliver better quality services and 72% would recommend products and services delivered by companies with clarity of Purpose to their friends.[36]

Being an activator of growth and a driver of profits, companies that operate with a clear and driving sense of Purpose outperform the S&P 500 by a factor of 10.[37] In their research Millward Brown and Jim Stengel developed a list of the worlds' 50 fastest growing brands out of 50,000 brands across 30+ countries (including both business to business (B2B) and business to consumer (B2C) businesses in 28 categories), which built the deepest relationships with customers and achieved the greatest financial growth. They found that investment in the companies that are able to serve a higher Purpose – the Stengel 50 – over a ten-year period would have been 400% more profitable than an investment in the S&P 500. Brands who center their businesses on ideals or a higher Purpose have a growth rate triple that of competitors in their categories.[38]. Kantar's Purpose 2020 study finds similar links: Purpose-driven brands grow twice as fast as their competition.[39]

Case in Point: Patagonia

Making Profits from Doing Good

Patagonia is a brand that leads by example when it comes to combining profits with Purpose. It manages its company and communications in accordance with the blueprint for durable business success in the 21st century. For Patagonia, corporate social responsibility and sustainable value creation are about aligning brand, Purpose and culture. Above all, this is a company that goes beyond words on such areas as mission, vision, values and core Purpose. Patagonia's ecosystem is synonymous with an organizational culture that actually lives these values and wills their vision into existence.

Patagonia's reason for being is about exploring nature without exploiting it. It is capitalist but not consumerist. Its mission was stated as "Build the best product, cause no unnecessary harm, and use business to inspire and implement solutions to the environmental crisis." The brand hasn't become Purpose-oriented recently. It has been so since the very beginning. In many ways it grows every time it amplifies its social mission. The annual growth rate of Patagonia sales has been well above industry-averages for most of the past 40 years.[40] As of 2018, Patagonia was worth $1 billion.[41]

Future competitive advantage is the result of genuine, long-term Purpose and profit orientation. In order for these dimensions to converge, cultural shifts are often needed. Purpose transformation differentiates in key aspects from general transformation initiatives. The latter are often top-down, cost-cutting ways to trim a company for better economic returns (profit) whilst the former embrace a more holistic approach, where profit is one – albeit important – part of transformation. Whilst hard to achieve, it is possible to retrofit Purpose thinking into almost any business.

When Purpose & Profit thinking converge, competitive advantage results

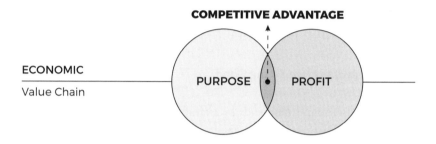

A strong set of arguments won't unite people, but a strong philosophy will. A rational model may be able to connect individuals, but a deeply rooted Purpose model is able to go beyond and offer a catalyst for a true cultural shift.

As a cultural reference, Ron Howard, director of a film about John Nash's endeavor called *A Beautiful Mind*, interpreted Nash's model in a scene showing his eureka moment. Nash in the movie expressed his discovery as follows: "Adam Smith said that the best result comes from everyone in the group doing what is best for himself, right? That's what he said. Incomplete. Because the best result would come from everyone in the group doing what is best for himself AND the group."

Organizational culture can only be cultivated and maintained if all stakeholders acknowledge the fact that the best results come from everyone in the group doing what is best for themselves AND the group. Research by IMD and Burson Cohn & Wolfe provides "strong evidence that leadership is a strong and consistent predictor of authentic corporate Purpose, explaining almost 50% of the variance in perceptions of authenticity."[42]

Purpose and profit are not opposites. Rather, the convergence of the two can help companies build long-term, sustainable ways to create competitive advantage. This is even more important in times when the concept of a unique selling proposition is increasingly a model of the past and when consumers and employees look for more than money in what they buy and do.

The world needs to see more industries and organizations genuinely adopt Purpose-driven leadership as part of their long-term thinking. It is for the good of companies, brands and their people. And whilst Purpose transformation needs to remain first and foremost an economic model for companies to build their future on, it is also a viable model that contributes to the good of our planet and the generations to come.

Few to all.
All to all.

Everywhere and Nowhere

"We are moving towards a new kind of augmented intelligence, defined by harnessing decision support systems and ambient computing that can support humans to solve problems individually and collectively that were previously beyond our capacity."

Sir Nigel Richard Shadbolt
Professor of Artificial Intelligence
University of Southampton

Technology that is everywhere all the time becomes invisible at some point. Mark D. Weiser, former chief scientist at Xerox said: "The most profound technologies are those that disappear. They weave themselves into the fabric of everyday life until they are indistinguishable from it." For the very first human beings on our planet, language was high technology. As time passed it became part of everyday life – invisible like oxygen, yet vital for survival. Similarly, electricity was once a luxury of the few, today it is everywhere and nowhere. Today, it is the digital era of zeros and ones that is omnipresent.

The fact that digital media is omnipresent in our lives has much to do with our physical environment. We were first introduced to Newtonian physics before we began exploring quantum physics. In the 21st century we are transitioning to the physics of information – a world that presents both challenges and opportunities we have yet to fully comprehend. When we talk about the physics of information, we essentially mean the laws underpinning the very notion of this transition. For instance, the omnipresence of hyperconnected digital media, enabled through fiber optics and free and superfast Wi- Fi, is a direct characteristic of what we would term the physics of information. According to Jay Walker-Smith at Yankelovich Consumer Research, we have gone from being exposed to about 500 ads a day back in the 1970s to as many as 5000 a day today.[43] It is almost overwhelming to consider the speed of this new physical reality. Nowadays, most things we do digitally are at the speed of light. It is a conundrum of sorts. We live in a fast, super-connected, and supposedly super-efficient world, but somehow, we still don't have time for anything. It is as if we are wasting more time to save time. As Tom Ford, the American designer and film director, stated: "Time and silence are the most luxurious things today."

There are more distractions than ever, more ways to be interrupted from whatever it is we are doing – a vibrating smartphone in your pocket, a loud TV commercial, a popup ad on your browser, an animated billboard on the street, nonstop WhatsApp or Snapchat pings that you simply can't ignore. Where does it end? In order to retain focus and keep balanced as human beings, but also as brands or businesses, we must develop critical skills to master our lives in this regard. Developing an optimum differentiation system is a way to improve the decision-making processes in times of information overload. It is a necessity to have a tool that helps us navigate through the new reality we live in today. Its key function: to cut through the clutter of choice and information that saturates our lives.

Historically speaking, knowledge was accessible only to the elite few and not yet democratized the way it is today. Yet, people always raised plenty of questions, which often led to revolutions. The fundamental issue was that people couldn't find answers to their questions. Today, however, not having answers is rare. The issue is more about asking the right question than finding the correct answer in the clutter of information. The modernist poet T.S. Eliot pondered this issue even before the age of digitalism: "Where is the wisdom we have lost in knowledge? Where is the knowledge we have lost in information?" It is as if we are drowning in information for craving knowledge. The hierarchy between information, knowledge and intelligence is illustrated in Figure 2, with intelligence being the least in quantity and the highest in quality. In this kind of environment, it is not those who have access to knowledge who will win, but those who gather the intelligence to develop their own informational navigation tool.

The new Know-How is the new Know-Why
(from information to intelligence)

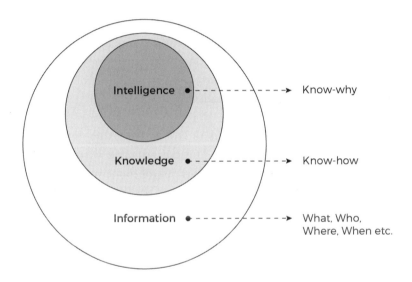

In an interview, communications analyst Marshall McLuhan explained: "There is in IBM, for example, a phrase: 'information overload produces pattern recognition' [...] When you give people too much information, they instantly resort to pattern recognition." It is not to say that this giant quantum leap forward of media and technology is wrong or right. Making value judgments when analyzing such grand shifts in civilization is not a pragmatic practice. Besides, it is too early for that. It is always smarter to simply stand back, break the paradigm into several parts and analyze it as systematically as possible in order to have a better view of the real zeitgeist of our times. There is no point in strategizing unless it is fully acknowledged that this present paradigmatic situation does, in fact, exist. Or in the words of Don Draper from *Mad Men*: "Change is not good or bad. It just is."

The more choice there is, the more difficult it is to decide. Aiming for clarity and cutting through the clutter is therefore a key skill to master in the 21st century. But it is harder than it sounds. It takes time to master and if your selection process is not underpinned by sound judgment, then the outcome of your decision will likely be suboptimal. So, how then do we optimize our choices?

To enhance our ability to make the right choice, whether personal or professional, we need to develop and embed a sort of automatism, an instinct for the right thing to do in any given situation.

The guiding Purpose principle is a mind's eye that allows you to keep your head above the flow of information rather than drown in it. Properly developed, it will yield clarity, help save time, streamline choices and increase the likelihood of making optimal decisions.

We'll use the subsequent chapters to look at contextual information and explore why the idea of a guiding Purpose principle is so central to our thinking, before moving on to the application of frameworks that will allow you to access the power of a *Guiding Purpose Strategy* for yourself and your brand. The ultimate goal is to help you develop your very own inner compass to navigate the future successfully.

We Are On Air

"The question isn't: 'What do we want to know about people?'
It's: 'What do people want to tell about themselves?'"

Mark Zuckerberg
Entrepreneur, Founder of Facebook

R&R Partners is probably best remembered for creating the campaign slogan 'What Happens in Vegas, Stays in Vegas.' A brilliant positioning claim that states that whatever happens during your visit, only happens there. And it happens far enough away not to have any negative effect on 'the here and now.'

Anyone born after 1985 and before 2005 is loosely termed a Millennial. Anyone born after 2005 will most likely fall into the category of Generation Z – a demographic that has yet to arrive into working life. Generational theory suggests significant changes across these bands (such as perspective on life, the attitude towards spending, belief and value systems etc.). However, it is most certainly the area of communication that leads to fundamental change in how we live. Up to Generation X (born after 1970 and before 1985), people mostly had one reality to contend with: *off the record*. The rapid evolution of technology has led to unprecedented change in how we communicate. Today, we essentially live in three different realities: *on the record, off the record* and a balanced blend of both, or what we will call an *amalgam* reality. Millennials and generations after them already live in these three realities simultaneously.

The idea of being *on the record* has always existed. However, the *on the record* reality used to be a mere representation or rather a piece of the *off the record* reality. It used to be just something that was recorded. Someone would say, "We are on air," which quite literally would refer to 'we are now being recorded' – a not so typical occasion. One would pay attention to what, how and where things would be 'recorded.' Fast forward several paradigms within the media and technology landscape and the *on the record* reality has broadened its meaning to include an entire world. It is now a dimension by itself and it is as big, if not bigger, than the *off the record* world.

We are witnessing the creation of a new normal in business culture, on an individual level and on a general sociocultural level, too. Anyone with teenage children will easily relate to how profound this shift is – accepting it as a new normality is even tougher. For many, being *off the record* feels dangerously uncomfortable as it implies being left out of the conversation. There are very few users of social media who use Facebook, Snapchat, Instagram and the like because they actually have something to say. The large majority of social media users are actively using it because they feel they *have to* say something.

It is essential to emphasize how dangerously easy it is today to be *on the record*. Simply by pulling a smartphone out of your pocket and tapping the screen with your finger, you are on air and *on the record*, most likely forever. This unprecedented ease of being *on the record* whenever, wherever, and whoever you are, has become one of the major driving forces of change in modern society. Anyone living in a democratic society has a voice, but, to be *on the record* in a matter of seconds and at your will, is beyond just having your voice heard. From a macroeconomic perspective, the communicative power has shifted to the consumer in an unparalleled way. This changes everything for brands, global organizations and firms, governments, authorities and so on.

There can be no doubt that this shift in how we live and perceive reality will lead to a much more fragmented, much more complex – but as we shall see later on, also a much more transparent – world. Therefore, we need to dig up the relevant contextual drivers in order to know how to create an appropriate map for this new reality before we can start navigating the future successfully.

Multiple Personality Order

"The meeting of two personalities is like the contact of two chemical substances: if there is any reaction both are transformed."

Carl Gustav Jung
Psychiatrist
Founder of Analytical Psychology

What are the implications of juggling three realities when it comes to one's personal and professional life? The three realities (*off the record, on the record* and *an amalgam of both*) mentioned in the previous chapter serve well to build a collective understanding of where total connectivity will likely propel us in the future. But how important will it be to have a real grasp of the implications? Where will the anticipated socioeconomic and sociocultural shifts lead us to?

Dissociative Identity Disorder (DID), better known as Multiple Personality Disorder (MPD), is a severe condition of the mind. The *Cambridge Dictionary of Psychology* defines it as follows:

> *n. A disorder characterized by the presence of two or more distinct personalities or identities in the same person who recurrently exchange control of the person and who may have*

only some knowledge about each other, and the history of the person involved.[44]

To be diagnosed with MPD is nothing pleasant. However, as our world becomes more fragmented and complex, one could argue that a new condition is emerging, particularly among younger generations. We refer to it as *Multiple Personality Order*. While we are not categorizing it as a clinical mental condition, it is no doubt akin in nature to a MPD.

Symptoms of a *Multiple Personality Order* are simultaneous expression of the three realities previously discussed – *off the record, on the record* and *an amalgam reality*. For each existence, there is a different personality and quite often, one's *on the record* self is vastly dissimilar to one's *off the record* counterpart. Anyone born and living before the early 1970s essentially grew up in a one-way communications world. Expressing oneself required a deliberate act such as writing a real, physical postcard, let's say, or perhaps owning a camcorder much later in life to create something to get *on the record* for a little while. Other than famous actors, singers, politicians or any other public figure, no one lived *on the record* permanently.

The evolution, if not the revolution, of media through technological advancements has provided us with the luxury to be on air, *on the record*, published online whenever we wish. What was once a major undertaking involving expensive equipment and hordes of savvy media professionals, is now achieved through a click on Facebook Live (or TikTok if you are 18 or younger). High-speed broadband combined with the very ease of appearing in a 'social newspaper,' (think of it as the Facebook newsfeed) has led to particular modes of behavior, attitudes and lifestyles. The idea of sharing one's choices and ways of living opens the gateway for creating new modes of existence.

We are not suggesting that millions of individuals have become popular celebrities. But it has suddenly turned millions of ordinary individuals into highly *médiatique* people who get more public exposure than any previous generation combined. Everyone can now leave a widely visible mark in history, or at least feel that they have. Essentially, self-expression and self-perception have spanned to an unprecedented extent, and the outcome is that status is no longer indicated merely through material wealth or by association with brands. It is also expressed through a public display of both verbal and visual information on individual experiences and feelings most often idealized towards the audience. The significance or insignificance of one's experiences and feelings is then determined by a thumbs-up or a thumbs-down. To be liked or not to be liked – that is the question.

Virtual and real worlds start to converge ever more. Many people are creating profiles in new channels and spending time, energy, and often capital, to develop them. At a certain stage, the profile starts to become a personality in and of itself, and eventually the online profile evolves as an additional personality. Perhaps the most prominent proxy to this idea is Second Life, a virtual world developed and owned by the San Francisco-based company Linden Lab. Second Life is similar to a massive multiplayer online role-playing game where users (also called residents) create virtual representations of themselves, called avatars, and are able to interact with places, objects, and other avatars. They can explore the world (known as the grid), meet other residents, socialize, participate in individual and group activities, build, create, shop, and trade virtual property and services with one another.[45] More recently, Fortnite by Epic Games takes the gamification (and addiction) levels to new heights, sporting an estimated 250 million interconnected players globally.[46]

An individual can organically make the transition into a dimension in which he or she might need to live out several personalities and know which one is appropriate in an online or a real-life situation. The implications of this state are related to maintaining a new kind of order – the *Multiple Personality Order*. From an individual's perspective, this order demands being well organized, maintained and managed. For anyone looking to 'sell' it, this means understanding that the approach to targeting and communicating with audiences has become a lot more complex. Brands and businesses can now target profiles and 'personalities' to reach consumers on a much more granular level. But, as we shall see, the transparency in this exchange goes both ways.

Values Across the Ages

*"Generational Value Systems explain how we got here
and where we're going"*

Graeme Codrington
Contributing Author, CEO of TomorrowToday
Speaker, Author and Advisor on the future of work.

There is a sociological framework that is really helpful in making sense of what can be an otherwise confusing moment in history: generational theory. Understanding generational value systems will help you to know why other people think and act the way they do, why younger and older people see the world so differently, and it will allow you to influence them by connecting with their value systems.

A 'value system' is a coherent set of beliefs and attitudes that influence every part of who we are and how we behave – also called 'worldviews' or 'paradigms.' Values are the deepest parts of what make us human, governing how we see the world and respond to it. It is values that help us decide what is right and wrong, good and bad, normal or weird. And they often work at a level below conscious thought – values help us make those snap judgments when we meet a new person, and they inform our major life decisions such as who to marry, how to handle death and what makes us happy.

Our value systems are shaped in the first two decades or so of our lives. We can gain insight into our own – and other people's – attitudes and actions by understanding the forces that shape our value systems. These include our religion, culture, gender, personality, education, economic status and social class.

One often-overlooked factor is the actual era in which each of us is born. This is what generational theory focuses on. We are all hugely influenced by the expectations and the norms of the society in which we grew up. Generational theory states that people born at a similar time in history, experiencing similar political, social and economic realities, educated in similar systems with similar curricula, and influenced by similar popular culture will develop similar worldviews. The theory looks for significant historical events in a country or region's history and identifies the impact these have on existing social orders and value systems. Sometimes these events result in the dawning of a new era, and therefore of new generational cohorts.

For example, from the late 1960s to the end of the 1980s, the world was in chaos. Everywhere. And then came a major tipping point. In 1989, Gorbachev came to power in Russia and announced Perestroika. In South Africa, de Klerk came to power and announced the ending of apartheid and the release of Mandela. In Romania, in 1989, the dictator Nicolae Ceauşescu was overthrown and Eastern Europe began to open up. In Germany, students punched the air with the global clenched fist 'power salute' as they danced on the Berlin Wall and smashed it to pieces – on '9/11' 1989. In China, earlier in 1989, students did the same on Tiananmen Square. And America invaded Panama in one of their 'pre-emptive strikes.' All this in 1989 – a tipping point in recent global history.

The generation of children born during the 1970s and 80s – the decades that led up to these tectonic shifts in global power – were greatly affected, developing an air of skepticism about adult control of the world, a sense of impermanence and a pragmatic view of power and power structures. These are the so-called "Generation Xers", who are now in midlife. They are pragmatic, self-reliant (to a fault), short-term focused, not really concerned about authority structures, informal, mobile, they need options and flexibility, they dislike close supervision, preferring freedom and an outputs-driven workplace. They love change so much they actually need it.

Of course, these are generalizations. But just like personality profiles, or gender-based analyses of people (such as the best-selling *Men are from Mars and Women are from Venus*), these generalizations can be useful as a starting point for understanding why someone behaves the way they do. For example, Generation Xers grew up as 'latchkey kids,' with their Baby Boomer parents giving them unprecedented levels of freedom of movement and freedom from supervision when they were young. They learnt to look after themselves. Now, as middle and senior managers, Gen Xers are very likely to be quite hands off. They don't like to be micromanaged, and they don't like to manage others very closely. The next generation – the Millennials – actually need more structure, more supervision and more management because they've been raised by helicopter parents in very structured school systems. It leads to a lot of frustration and mismatched expectations at work. Gen Xers think they're doing a great job by saying "Here's what I need done, but I am not going to impose any methods or management on you." But Millennials feel they've not been given enough support and have been set up to fail.

Those Millennials – or Generation Y – are the generation of children born after the era changing events of 1989. And they have a very different view of the world. Also, 1989 was the year that Tim Berners-Lee created the hypertext protocol that gave us websites as we know them today. Not only was it the dawning of the internet age, the 1990s also saw the emergence of Microsoft and cellphones. Children of the 1990s and 2000s have grown up digital – they're digital natives, if you like; whereas older people are digital immigrants (with a few digital dinosaurs still roaming around too).

Millennials are idealistic rather than pragmatic. They believe that they can change the world – and they believe they have to. Today's teens and 20-somethings see a world struggling with a variety of issues from racism and gender-based violence to climate change and depleted natural resources, and they want to get involved and make a difference. They have a sense of civic duty and responsibility; they are connected, global in their mindset and embrace diversity, with an innovative and entrepreneurial mindset that will take them far.

Generational theory has an elegant simplicity to it. Unlike more complex segmentation tools, generational theory is immediately applicable. This understanding of different generations and the 'gap' between them has many applications in all areas of life, from parents interacting with children, to salespeople selling to younger or older clients, to managers who work with teams of people of different ages. By understanding the impact of different generations, inside and outside your organization, you can improve customer relationships, and the productivity and interactions of your teams. Just by knowing someone's age, you can adjust your approach to them and have a greater chance of connecting with them, and therefore influencing them.

Even more valuable, using generational theory we can predict how the generations will grow up. We can look back at the way in which older, and still living generations have grown up and what they are like today, based on the influences they experienced in their youth. We can then postulate about the different influences on today's young people, and how they might be affected as they grow up through the predictable life stages every generation must go through.

Back in 1999, I predicted that Generation X would not produce many – if any – significant political leaders. At that time, we were seeing the Baby Boomers finally start to take power, with many young leaders stepping onto national stages (think Clinton, Blair and Putin). I predicted that this generation would keep hold of power until well into the 2020s, when they pass the baton to the Millennials – skipping Gen X entirely. I remain convinced that this will be the pattern. Gen X is just not interested in organizational power and structural authority.

Generation gurus Neil Strauss and William Howe summarize the predictive power of generational theory this way: "History creates generations, and generations create history. The cycle draws forward energy from each generation's need to redefine the social role of each new phase of life it enters. And it draws circular energy from each generation's tendency to fill perceived gaps and to correct (indeed, overcorrect) the excesses of its elders."

Today's young people are definitely not just younger versions of today's old people. A significant change in societal values is underway. And you can see this in all parts of the world, not just the suburbs of rich, Western nations.

This is where generational theory is at its most powerful – and most valuable. It reminds us to focus on values when we communicate and engage with people. If it is our value systems that ultimately determine how we see the world, how we act and react, and how we measure the success of our lives, then it is no wonder that the idea of being 'values based' is becoming more and more important in our world. When we tap into the core values of different generations, we speak not to just the head and heart, but the soul as well. And this is when we are at our most effective in influencing others.

Leaders who understand the power of values need to also understand that different generations perceive and engage with values in different ways. Yes, there are enduring human values that have lasted across the eras of history. But each generation engages with these values in different ways, and we cannot take a one-size-fits-all approach to the way in which we communicate or implement values in our organizations, teams or families.

The Opinion Economy

*"It is one of the ironies of history
that people who live through a revolution are least likely to understand it.
Nor do we realize where it comes from, where it is taking us,
and where the various currents within it find their roots."*

Dr Jacques Fabrice Vallee
Computer Scientist
Co-developer of ARPANET
(a precursor to the internet)

Aristotle concluded that pleasure is the only intrinsic good in life and therefore, it must be the ultimate Purpose to pursue. Life's aim was postulated as maximizing pleasure and minimizing pain. Because we derive pleasure from helping others, we can assume that if everyone maximizes pleasure, life would ultimately be good for everyone. Jeremy Bentham took this a step further with his 'Rule of Utility', stating that "good is whatever brings the greatest happiness to the greatest number of people." Advocating this on a collective level is what drives ethical behavior in our society.

The problem with this approach is subjectivity. Who decides what is best for all? Who decides what happiness is in the first place? If the power to decide over a question like this is left to a sole, or even a few, individuals, then the outcome can potentially be disastrous. Human history has taught us a lesson or two bearing many examples of dictators and autocrats who chose what was good for them rather than what was good for the people. In terms of branding, this 'few to all' model is no longer relevant.

Collective Connectivity

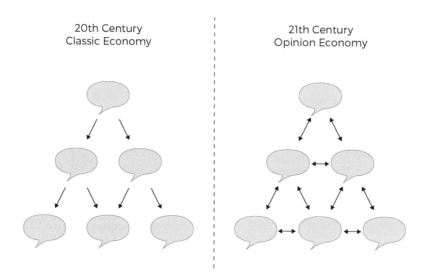

| 20th Century Classic Economy | 21th Century Opinion Economy |

UNICEF estimates that an average of 353,000[47] babies are born each day. Apple sells quite consistently about 75 million[48] iPhones in the first quarter of each calendar year. That makes for about 827,000 iPhones each day – and Apple isn't alone. At about 20%[49] of the market, this translates to a ratio of about 11 smart phones on the grid for every baby being born. In the time it took you to read from the beginning of this chapter to this paragraph, about 100 babies were born – and over 1000 more people are now connected to the world of wireless communication – on iPhones alone.

Today consumers have unprecedented access to technology that can make their voices heard. More and more individuals are joining the world's media ecosystem. Word of mouth, the oldest medium and certainly still effective by any means, is becoming the strongest again. It is *the* medium of today and tomorrow.

Consequently, the power has been placed into the hands of consumers – almost regardless of how much money a company invests in marketing. Pernod Ricard's former CMO Martin Riley summed the dynamic up quite nicely: "Any ill-thought through commercial promotion in Thailand or Peru can come back and bite you in the UK or Australia. Today, brands are only as strong as their weakest link."[50] In other words, thanks to a plethora of apps, we have long moved from simple price checks on-the-go, to a state of impacting the economy in much more fundamental ways, changing the very nature of how value is created – or destroyed.

The concept of *Multiple Personality Order* as outlined in the previous chapter can make the alternative ego of a consumer inspire or perhaps conspire a movement against a certain brand or business. The potential is already there, and it would only take a few rebellious characters to trigger viral chaos. "Research shows that 90% of consumers would boycott a company if they learnt about any irresponsible business practices."[51] The 'project mayhem' that evolved out of *Fight Club*[52] would target a specific corporation by influencing the opinions of the corporations' clientele and staff. The film's main message is that the inner world of the protagonist was created to add Purpose to his meaningless life of sameness, boredom, routine and monotony. In reality, it is even easier for the connected consumer to develop a rebellious alternative ego in an ordered context than in a disordered one. In today's digital age, as Martin Riley warned, every brand can have its own "Tahrir Square or WikiLeaks moment." Eric Schmidt (Google's CEO from 2001 to 2011) put it quite eloquently: "The Internet is the first thing that humanity has built that humanity doesn't understand, it is the largest experiment in anarchy that we have ever had."

Entire value chains are changing. The commentary section on Amazon influences the purchase of books and much more. The opinions and ratings on Yelp or TripAdvisor have become the most important determining factor when choosing a restaurant, cafe or a place to stay. The prettiest picture or the coolest brand video cannot repair the damage of negative ratings on these platforms. In times when a simple click or scan of a barcode is enough to compare pricing and service offers, the most fundamental marketing principles need to be called into question. However, the opinion of one individual has limited value. It is the aggregation of opinions that creates real power. Whatever you market, the only way to create and sustain value over time is to make sure you deliver integrity and value inside out.

Supply chain management was an offspring of the industrial revolution: building systems to make processes more efficient. In our times, supply chain management is about value systems and transparency. Sourcemap, for instance, was one of the first platforms created for supply chain transparency across sectors ranging from pharmaceuticals to electronics. Leo Bonanni, CEO of Sourcemap, once claimed that "there are no remaining technical barriers to supply chain traceability."[53] As consumers we are no wiser than before. It is just that today it takes little or no effort to see if a promise of a better and cheaper product holds true. You don't need to have exclusive connections to the secret service to view the profile, prices or ratings of a particular brand, product or company. For the first time, businesses, brands and people are more likely to get caught in a lie or will be exposed for half-truths.

Marketing communications used to connect brands with consumers. Now consumers are connected to each other, so it doesn't really matter what you tell your customers on your website or on your commercials. Critical success factors such as positioning, differentiation, claiming a specific territory in the minds of customers will continue to preserve their key role in the discipline of brand building, but the means to achieve these have changed forever. Asking an advertising agency to do the makeup or polishing of a flawed proposition won't work. Brushing a bit of CSR (Corporate Social Responsibility) paint over an annual report of a company that delivers super low prices at the cost of exploiting people in another corner of the world is shortsighted.

Fish can't see water. The issue is that most of us fail to see the ongoing revolution of the opinion economy because we are so caught up in it. For people, brands and businesses, it is not just a matter of being honest. It is also about recognizing the changing context. Connecting everyone with everybody (web), everybody with everything (IoT or Internet of Things) and everything with everything (Industry 4.0) marks only the beginning of what the opinion economy has in store for us. We believe that when value chains become totally transparent, power will be decentralized. Making way for the coming era of *radical transparency* – rapid, aggregated and (decentralized) validated exchange of opinions – for better or worse.

The Viral Spiral

"Profit in business comes from repeat customers, customers that boast about your project or service, and that bring friends with them."

Dr W. Edwards Deming
Statistician and Management Consultant

When a brand is driven by its core Purpose and reaches the 'cult' stage for a group of consumers, it lends itself to an often underrated medium: *word of mouth*. It sounds old-fashioned, but in essence, it is still the most organic and most powerful medium to opt for. At best, it neither looks like an advertisement, nor does it sound like one. Creative Director and Founder of Doyle Dane Bernbach (DDB), William Bernbach asserts that "Word of mouth is the best medium of all." According to Nielsen's Global Trust in Advertising Report, 92% of the 28,000 internet respondents surveyed trust recommendations from friends and family above all other forms of advertising.[54]

By growing a brand in a transparent and coherent way, protecting the trust built between the audience and the brand, early adopters can become the most influential advocates to carry a brand's inner workings and spread the news to more people. Harley-Davidson is perhaps the epitome of how powerful the effects of word of mouth can work over time. But emerging from near bankruptcy at the end of the seventies to achieve cult status, where fans tattoo the brand's logo onto their bodies, requires more than a radiant brand-core. It took a management team that recognized how to build an entire world around the brand's core. They understood that building passion for the brand meant more than riding a motorcycle from point A to point B.

Consumers who belong to the group of early adopters voluntarily promote a brand's values and spread the word about products and services with authentic passion. Joining the early adopters are the loyalists who may have made late purchases but nonetheless feel a strong bond, so long as a brand stays loyal its overarching Purpose.

Loyalists, much like early adopters, become ambassadors and representatives of a brand, and most often even play the role of secret agents. They begin to distribute positive intelligence, so to speak, about a brand – driven and motivated by an unspoken agreement. The beauty of this is that it never interrupts, disturbs or distracts attention. It is always within a contextual setting or mise-en-scène. In short, brand ambassadors deliver your message in the right place at the right time and often to the right people. We call this effect 'accessing the viral spiral.'

The most advanced stage of this craft of ambassadorship can be observed within the luxury goods sector. Whilst word of mouth is known and discussed in standard marketing, it hardly makes it to the priority list of today's marketing strategies. It is recognized as being powerful, but hard to achieve. It is much easier (and often faster) to spend marketing budgets on big campaigns to convince the masses.

Luxury brands, on the other hand, have been successfully running word-of-mouth strategies since the 17th century. In fact, it is still considered the best of mediums today, because the product, or object of desire to put it more correctly, is always so perfect that it advertises itself. Indeed, the luxury industry does not see 'Marketing' as a discipline worth pursuing. Rather, it adheres to the so-called 'Anti Laws of Marketing,'[55] which we shall see later on, provide interesting perspectives on how to win the hearts of audiences.

In 1833 when Aleksander Pushkin published his novel *Eugene Onegin* in verse, it was one of the most read works among the high society circles of St. Petersburg. In this iconic novel, Pushkin positions a luxury brand:

> *A dandy on the boulevards, [...] strolling at leisure until his*
> *Breguet, ever vigilant, reminds him it is midday.*

This particular product placement was made without a commercial agreement. It is important to emphasize that back then, there was no such thing as the advertising or marketing industry. Pushkin featured a Breguet timepiece in what has become a classic work of Russian literature simply because he shared the same fascination with luxury watchmaking as did Russia's high society. Today, Breguet proudly uses this literary reference in their brand communications to great effect, associating the brand with poetic prestige. Genuine luxury brands cater to a small but lucrative niche market of expert customers. Like Harley-Davidson, these brands have masterfully created a brand-core that captivates people to such a degree that they willingly become influencers and advocates for the brand.

The advent of social media has brought us word of mouth on steroids. As we are on the verge of an opinion economy boom, this particular medium is now more relevant than ever. In this kind of economy, customers are influenced by brands only at a metalevel, and increasingly rely on 'peers' to make purchase decisions (or in marketing-speak: 'Influencers'). Mass communication is no longer from few to all. It has become all to all. Not only do consumers get information about your firm from your website, let alone from a close friend next door, but also from the aggregate experiences and ratings of unknown consumers around the world. Who would have ever thought that we would trust the opinion of someone living halfway across the globe and whom we've never even met – in other words, a total stranger? This very dynamic implies a paradigm shift in which the roles and rules of the game have changed fundamentally. As Scott David Cook, co-founder of Intuit and a director of Procter & Gamble put it: "A brand is no longer what you tell consumers it is, it is what they tell each other it is."

Word of mouth functions as social proof and it triggers the viral spiral. It has to do with who recommends your brand or firm and lends it the legitimacy it needs to be underpinned with credibility. It is about getting positive references from those affiliated with relevant clients, partners, stakeholders, teams, consumer segments, etc. Word of mouth is still the only medium of direct interpersonal interaction, both *on the record* and *off the record*. It is important to remember that a word of mouth strategy is not only beneficial for B2C (Business to Consumer) marketing but also and in particular for B2B (Business to Business) marketing. In fact, analysis shows that business buyers are influenced by direct interactions with suppliers much more than anything else.[56]

Indeed, word of mouth is more influential today due to the rapid rise of social media and because company driven marketing is mostly limited to the initial stages in the purchase journey. Traditional marketing is by no means less important, but when it comes to purchasing decisions, the power of influence is truly unleashed through word of mouth and its digital equivalents. Through the rise of the opinion economy, consumers no longer decide on brands and products as linearly as they used to do.[57] It seems as though the closer we get to the point of purchasing, the more we look to others to inform and even approve our final decision.

Startups generally don't have the same astronomical budgets as the global behemoths do. David Rusenko, the co-founder and CEO of the web hosting company Weebly said: "Word-of-mouth marketing is a crucial component of organic growth for startups and one of the primary ways that Weebly has grown to over 15 million customers." This medium is the engine that creates buzz, viral communication and endless referrals. But which brands have consistently been able to use the word of mouth medium throughout history? Generally speaking, it is the companies and entrepreneurs that define their core Purpose early on and then ruthlessly pursue it over time. A great proxy to look for input in this area is the luxury industry. Take Brunello Cucinelli's Purpose of 'humane capitalism,' for instance. His genuinely 'made in Italy' luxury fashion label not only pays employees up to 20% more than the industry average, but staff members do not have to punch time clocks, nor are they expected to answer after-hours emails – in fact, it is not allowed. The company also donates 20% of its profits to a charitable cause.[58]

The *Guiding Purpose Strategy* creates clients who create clients. It doesn't buy an audience but builds audiences that build audience. A deeply connected, inner clarity for who you are and what you stand for is critical to accessing the viral spiral. The phenomenon of all-to-all communication is an indicator of the fact that the viral spiral is as great of an opportunity as it is a danger. To put it in the words of Dr Jef I. Richards: "While it may be true that the best advertising is word-of-mouth, never lose sight of the fact it also can be the worst advertising."

Purpose Perspectives

Don't Hide Behind the Brand

*"Unlike grownups, children have little need
to deceive themselves."*

Johann Wolfgang von Goethe
German Writer and Statesman

In embracing the zeitgeist, it is easy to see complexity accelerating at a pace difficult to keep up with. If you or your organization is successful today, you need to be mindful of the fact that what got you here, won't get you there. However difficult it may seem, it is actually helpful to abandon conventional business thinking and detach from reality as we see it, even if it is for just a brief moment.

The luxury industry is definitely the place in which to look for brand power beyond the simple valuation of a brands' ability to capture people's attention (and wallets). Astute luxury brand managers are virtuosos when it comes to merging the intangible with the tangible to create desirability for their brands. Fueled with dreams and aspirations, these brands deliberately play with the risk of not serving certain clients. They often pick a positioning that is polarizing at the cost of excluding certain market segments. Luxury brands also play with pricing, often increasing prices over time. The one constant in the equation is brand. Because the brand is loaded with meaning and carries weight, it consistently earns the loyalty and trust of customers. A luxury brand commands authority and is respected rather than liked.

The reason why many mainstream brands fail to add value to their brand is rooted in the belief that 'brand' as an asset will do the work for the product. Or in other words: that investing in massive marketing campaigns is better than investing in the improvement of the product – which of course is a complete delusion. Although it is still observable in the non-luxury sector, there is really no need to invest astronomical sums on mass marketing. The product or service is one of the essential manifestations of the brand and when developed with meticulous care, it will create a pull. This does not just relate to quality, but to innovation as well. Think of Apple or Tesla. These companies have taught us that when you metamorphose and transform a product into an object of desire, it begins to sell itself, creating a rather nice dynamic of demand outstripping supply.

Not long-ago transparency was just another fancy word used in business terminology. Investing millions in mass marketing does not necessarily mean investing in the brand as a whole. If anything, you are helping the marketing industry grow instead of helping your brand grow. Those days of hiding behind the brand are over. Producing weak products or delivering shallow service levels under the cover of a strong brand will not bode well with consumers – they can see you!

Today's consumers and those of the future will no longer trust corporate messaging in the way they used to. They turn elsewhere to learn the truth, searching instantly online to find out if a product has quality issues or if a company has been exposed for unethical behavior. You can shut down TV programs or censor print media, but online media is frequented by people acting as independent, investigative journalists armed with smartphones – and they are unstoppable in both speed and scale. The documentary *The Naked Brand*, demonstrates impressively how there are more videos uploaded on YouTube in a month than the major TV networks have broadcast in the last 60 years combined.[59]

Supply chain management is being transformed on a fundamental level. Brands can no longer shift the blame onto other parts of the value chain. Connectivity and transparency have left companies and their brands no choice but to take full responsibility for their oil spills, child labor, mistreatment of animals and so on.

Total connectivity and radical transparency are changing the very nature of competition as well. Many of us still remember Toyota's failure to admit its faults. What started as a single, horrifying car accident in southern California, eventually turned into a global vehicle recall and the sales suspension of eight of Toyota's best-selling models, a move that cost the company and its dealers a whopping US$54 million a day in lost sales revenue.[60] In addition to financial losses, the story that ensued was one of denial. Toyota failed to take responsibility, which shook the solid foundation of trust the company had so painstakingly built up by producing good quality cars over many decades. Toyota as a brand was completely exposed, showing the world that it preferred to invest more time and capital on marketing than on safety.

Or think of Volkswagen, triggering one of the greatest scandals in automotive history by deliberately manipulating data. The engine software was manipulated to "detect when cars were being tested, changing the performance accordingly to improve (emissions) results."[61] Making customers believe they were buying an environmentally friendly car for the benefit of gaining competitive advantage was short-lived, as the company failed to take value-chain transparency into account. The German car company operated in a near dictatorial fashion, destroying its own solid reputation, losing one third of its market value in a matter of days. According to Burson-Marsteller's research, 40% of a company's reputation is driven by Purpose.[62] When Purpose and the behavior of an organization are too far apart, reputation – the currency of our times – is shattered and profits decrease.

Some of our world's corporations are bigger than countries. Considering the fact that almost half of the world's top 100 largest economic entities are corporations, it is time for corporate leaders to acknowledge the reality that they have as much responsibility for the world's future as their non-corporate peers do.[63] It is time to start investing more time, energy and capital in Purpose and the ensuing culture if you are serious about investing in the future. A bigger marketing budget will not necessarily lead to an increase in brand value. The real opportunity lies in mastering the ability to be a totally transparent brand that is aligned with a deeper Purpose. Repairing a negative image will become irrelevant as the new strategic approach focuses on preventing negative reputation in the first place. This is where the opportunity is long term. Brands that are aligned with their higher Purpose will stand the test of time, as they connect with their audiences and build trust from within. In keeping a solid consumer rapport, one becomes automatically attuned to the signs of the future.

Signs From The Future

"Any sufficiently advanced technology is equivalent to magic."

Sir Arthur C. Clarke
British Author, Futurologist
and Science Writer

Many of the devices we use today were depicted in sci-fi films such as *Star Wars*, *Minority Report*, *Star Trek*, *Avatar* and so forth. In 1865, Jules Verne wrote *From the Earth to the Moon*. What was total fiction back then turned out to be an indication of where the world was headed. Then he wrote *Twenty Thousand Leagues Under the Sea* in 1870, the source of inspiration for the inventor of the submarine. Verne then went on to envision the helicopter in *Nautilus*. Clearly, such fictional stories and their heroes have spurred creativity and inventiveness in the great minds of our times. Take Martin Cooper, the director of research and development at Motorola, for example. He credited the *Star Trek* communicator for the design of the first mobile phone in the early 1970s. "That was not fantasy to us," Cooper said, "that was an objective."[64]

Sir Arthur C. Clarke wrote about 'Geostationary Satellite Communications,' which basically meant online networks. Google glass reminds us of the *Terminator* who could immediately create a profile of the person he just met. Space travel, which has been the main subject of several sci-fi films, is becoming a branch of the tourism business today. Numerous other visionary authors, including H.G. Wells, Aldous Huxley and Isaac Asimov foresaw the inventions of our modern world. The astonishing and fascinating side of this continuing pattern is that these authors have the ability to illustrate such future advances of science in meticulous detail using the limited language of the times they live in. It is certainly a sound argument to say that stories authored by visionaries often pre-paint the future.

Karel Čapek, the Czech writer, was the first to introduce and popularize the frequently used international word robot. There is an abundance of films on robots that go beyond the man vs robot theme and address the emerging relationship between humanity and robotics or humanity and artificial intelligence (e.g. *Her*, *Ex Machina*, *Bicentennial Man*, *A.I. Artificial Intelligence*, etc.). These works communicate the signs of the future and how technological advancements could influence our lives, our behavior and our society.

We are witnessing the intensity and scale of scientific achievements in the field of robotics advancing at high speed. We already have self-operating vacuum cleaners, industrial factory robots, military robots, smart drones and so on. Boeing, Google and Boston Robotics are some of the leading brands pursuing the robotics industry in multiple directions.

According to futurists, some of the devices we've seen in the films of the last decade will likely become part of our daily reality in a shorter period of time than most people think. Moore's Law, for example, states that computer power doubles every 18 months. The key is to identify which authors are authorities in using their imagination. What's relevant for the new generation of entrepreneurs are the subtleties that these futuristic authors sprinkle through their masterpieces. Their imagination is not limited to future inventions but rather encompasses the future of business and science. They give thought to how human relationships with science will change and with artistic license ask questions that are perhaps taboo among scientists, engineers and entrepreneurs. In the artistic space they can introduce the intangible that precedes the tangible. Marshall McLuhan, the Canadian communications analyst and futurist said: "It has always been the artist who perceives the alterations in man caused by a new medium, who recognizes that the future is the present and who uses his work to prepare the ground for it." We need the artists, maestros and the creatives to help us set the foundation for the future of business, science and civilization in general.

There are several other sources of inspiration to draw from to spice up your company, your brand or even yourself. Many strategists, managers and business leaders take these sources for granted. Lidewij Edelkoort, a Dutch futurist and design forecaster said: "Suddenly mythology and iconography are relevant sources of inspiration and at the core is this study of contemporary archetypes, drawing upon muses and models and oracles to design a future of fashion with a gentle and elegant hand." We have been receiving signs from the future for thousands of years. The trick is staying alert and open to them. Budding app creators, fin-tech entrepreneurs and scientists working on the developments of quantum computing and nanotechnology must broaden their minds in order to recognize these.

The R&D world of today refuses to take the word 'impossible' seriously. For instance, the notion of time travel, specifically travelling to the future faster than others, was absolutely inconceivable. Now it can be explained through quantum science. According to the Pentagon, by 2045 people will communicate using neural activity alone.[65] This means that what we consider as magic today will become the norm of tomorrow. There has been more change for humanity in the last 100 years than in the last one million years combined.

Failing to recognize the macro-shifts in the value systems may not be a problem for your organization in the next five years, but it will be a problem in the next two decades ahead of us. In specific sectors and countries, not recognizing Purpose or failing to make it a priority may very well put you out of business in the 2040s. The implications on strategy are huge, particularly for companies with long-term planning cycles such as UBS, BP, etc., anticipating scenarios for the next 50 years on issues such as how to source energy, for instance.

The luxury industry is the only industry that has always belonged to the Purpose club. Technology, media and automotive industries will most likely join before the finance industry. Private sectors in mature economies have already begun taking steps in the right direction. Some of the emerging countries are also making their way to the club, although many still operate on basic transactional value for lack of choice and progress in certain industries. The Edelman Good Purpose Study found that "62% of consumers in Rapid Growth Economies (RGEs) purchase products with Purpose at least monthly."[66]

Applying Moore's Law loosely to the speed of change in organizations, Purpose-led transformation will enter our lives a lot quicker than we think. One can argue that this macro-shift will be equivalent to an industrial revolution in its intensity and scope.

Expect the Unexpected

*"Innovation is the whim of an elite
before it becomes a need of the public."*

Ludwig von Mises
Austrian School Behavioral Economist

Growth can take many forms. Hence, it is worth taking a moment to step back and reflect on how we can identify where growth is most likely to come from. Future economic growth on a macro level for example can be better understood by looking at the large industry consolidation cycles and the global rhythms of history. A basic model of industry evolution can help us understand not only where we are within our own sector, but what likely dynamics will shape our future.

The authors Deans, Kroeger and Zeisel[67] put the idea forward that essentially every industry undergoes four major phases. The starting position (Stage 1) is equivalent to a gold-rush era: real or perceived opportunity attracts many new players and a lot of money into the market. What used to be the mushrooming and nascent automotive industry at the turn of the 20h century for instance, is today the rapid rise of AI and tech companies.

The Industry Consolidation Cycle

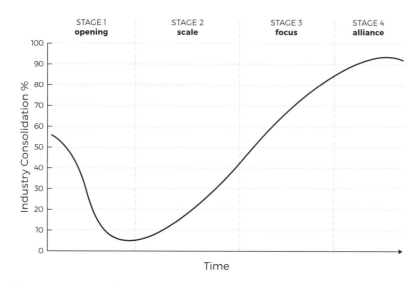

To continue on this example: as car companies started to scale their business (Stage 2) and optimize their processes (Stage 3), the industry started to consolidate fiercely. From over 500 car manufacturing companies in the US alone, only three giants and its sub brands were left at the end of this cycle: Ford, General Motors and Chrysler. Today, the automotive industry is beyond consolidation and shapes alliances (Stage 4) in order to still innovate and create IP that allows them to move forward. However, the industry consolidation lifecycle theory also states that at the end of Stage 4, an industry is ripe for disruption. Or, in other words, it either reinvents itself or it disappears altogether. The automotive industry for one is fighting hard as its future is most uncertain. The great revolution is not in propulsion (the first electric car, the Flocken Elektrowagen, dates back to 1888), but to the very concept of mobility. And the latter is no longer about wheels, but about how we spend our time in an era of total connectivity, where the need to physically move from one location decreases. One strategy is to invest and look for innovation outside your home turf. BMW for instance created a venture capital fund of over half a billion USD with the sole Purpose to react faster to trends and nascent capabilities that will shape the space of mobility and which the company cannot build fast enough inhouse.[68]

The question of course, is one of orientation. Where is our industry heading, where are we heading and how will we remain relevant in the future?

The leading edge and state-of-the-art paradigm in regard to future growth belongs to those who are ahead. As the Hungarian-American physicist Edward Teller famously said: "Today's science is tomorrow's technology." No matter how much people associate technology with science, the two are very different fields. Scientific research is much more long-term and deeper than today's technology. Formula 1 is ahead of the high-end supercars. Academia is ahead of commerce. Secret service agencies are ahead of embassies. Many diplomats are ahead of the politicians.

But not all growth is good. Especially when we look at the potential impact speed (acceleration) can have in combination with technological evolution. Criticism is growing from luminaries such as Elon Musk, Prof. Stephen Hawking and Prof. Yuval Harari who all indicate that Artificial Intelligence and Autonomous Technologies need to be regulated. It's important to note that these individuals are far from being associated from governments or regulatory authorities. Their collective claim can loosely be interpreted as that when artificial intelligence lacks the intelligence to wait until it is given permission or authorization to be so, then it may outpace us before we have the chance to handle it properly.

There have been numerous discussions, analyses, papers and conferences on the demographic consequences of future growth, but little or no thought has been given to the psychographic consequences thereof. When we look at the brief history of civilizations' chronological development, we can see that technological progress (i.e. toolmaking) is linked to population growth. Revealing the data of their study, Dr Jacques Vallee and Prof. Francois Meyer argue that there is a positive feedback mechanism linking technological development and population. As Meyer and Vallee wrote: "The demographic growth of the species (…) does not follow an exponential development curve with a constant rate, but a hyper-exponential law with increasing rate."[69]

The fantastic UFOs of yesterday are the autonomous drones of today being already used in agriculture, delivery services and in the military. The well-connected fridge knows what you are running out of or what will soon expire, transferring this data anonymously to your choice of supermarket and triggering a delivery for you; reducing complexity and consumerist waste.

So then, what does the future hold in regard to growth? There cannot be any doubt that an elaborate answer to this question will fill a book (or more likely, several volumes) in its own right. What we do know is that the only constant is change, and it happens at an exponential rate. May we suggest holding two thoughts. Firstly, growth will likely occur in areas we expect it the least. And secondly, in an environment of rapid growth, complexity tends to increase and so does the yearning for simplification and meaning.

Reducing Pain and Maximizing Pleasure

"The good is whatever brings the greatest happiness
to the greatest number of people."

Jeremy Bentham
British Philosopher, Jurist and Social Reformer

Many Eastern and Western philosophers in ancient times dedicated their lives to works that dealt with the philosophy of happiness. Hedonism is a school of thought built on this philosophy. Having a meaningful life guided by an inner Purpose that serves both the individual and the society is one of the most effective ways to successfully achieve and maintain a hedonistic lifestyle. Purpose-led entrepreneurs are already running new startups based on a hedonist agenda of making profit whilst contributing to the wellbeing of society. Where will this Purpose-led transformation make an impact first?

There is no doubt that health will be a macro-theme in the future. Medical science will become more precise and treat patients according to their physiological structure instead of treating everyone in the same way. While science may be objective, human beings are not all the same. Some have stronger bodies, while others have phobias and fears. Tasso Inc., an American startup, is already well advanced in its development of a device called Hemolink, which draws blood samples in a needle-free way. Hemolink collects enough blood for a broad range of diagnostic applications and connects seamlessly to trusted laboratories. Similar to the way Google personalizes your search results, your medical procedures will also be personalized according to your physiological and psychological structure. These are examples of companies with Purpose-driving progress in the field of medical science for the benefit of all.

Forward-thinking hospitals have made the firm decision to design their interior in the same fashion as luxury hotels – elegant and equipped with an entire sensory-experiential atmosphere. Several studies demonstrate that the design inside clinical settings can have a positive impact on patient outcomes.[70] Behavioral economics can explain how a classy interior design can reduce pain to the extent that the patients will want to stay longer even after they are actually healed. The hospital world wisely continues to learn from the world of luxury.

Dr Viktor Frankl, Austrian psychiatrist, neurologist and a key figure in existential therapy, explained how finding meaning could heal. As a Holocaust survivor, his experiences in the concentration camp were proof that finding meaning even in the most brutal situations helps one say yes to life. Surviving and escaping from that camp seemed statistically impossible for him – but finding meaning and Purpose in life helped him hold on to the very small possibility of surviving. Later during his career, he published a book called *Man's Search for Meaning* in which he describes his experiences and how he came to believe in Purpose-oriented therapy.

In later decades, as Nick Craig and Scott A. Snook wrote, "doctors have even found that people with Purpose in their lives are less prone to disease."[71] A study, conducted by researchers at Rush University Medical Center in Chicago found that "participants with high scores on the life Purpose test were 2.4 times less likely to develop Alzheimer's compared with those who had the lowest scores."[72] There is plenty of evidence on how being driven by a higher Purpose is not only good for psychological health but also for physical health. In 2015, the Mount Sinai Medical Center conducted a study that showed that a high sense of Purpose is associated with a 23% reduction in death from all causes and a 19% risk reduction of heart attacks, strokes, or the need for coronary artery bypass surgery. The research team reviewed ten relevant studies with the data of more than 137,000 people to analyze the impact of sense of Purpose on death rates and risk of cardiovascular events. The meta-analysis also found that those with a low sense of Purpose are more likely to die or experience cardiovascular events.[73]

On a fundamental level, it will not be about technological progress in and of itself. More likely, it will all depend on the Purpose of the world's inventors in developing the next wave of technological means. The goal will be not only to heal patients, but also to prevent or eliminate diseases and viruses. The future of health will focus on achieving the physical health of individuals and improving the overall wellbeing of civilizations, simultaneously reducing pain and maximizing pleasure in the process. Taking into account the Fourth Industrial Revolution, Stewart Wallis from the New Economics Foundation aptly stated: "History tells us that a value shift is triggered by creation of a new story about how we want to live."

Doing Well Matters

"What drives good change is our collective motivation to do better."

Willi Helbling
Contributing Author, Chief Executive Officer,
Business Professionals Network

Every form of economic activity is based on values, norms and an understanding of what meaningful action is. Economic activity means 'creating value.' Value creation raises the question of the practicability (as in 'quality of life') of the values to be created. This is one of the core questions of progressive, industrial societies. The socioeconomic questions and problems of our present time make it necessary to reflect on economic action: economic reason cannot do without questions of legitimation, responsibility and meaning. This debate can be followed daily in media – prominent examples are, or rather, were 'Dieselgate' at Volkswagen or 'Brent Spar' at Shell.

With every action comes a consequence. Underlying is however always an assumed level of trust and faith in the meaning of every action. Today, trust is questioned in every action, especially within an economic context. For example, by a distorted liberalism through which an often-visionless economy 'turns souls upside down.'[74] Responsible entrepreneurial action should increasingly be viewed from a perspective that goes beyond the actual business activity of a company.

Digital communication systems as well as the exuberant mobility of people and products infiltrate every corner of the globe. When everything is connected to everything, everything inevitably competes with everything. But pumping out more products and more connectivity does not automatically lead to higher value and better, inner enrichment, but often to reduced living possibilities for future generations. If we are not careful, the dynamics at play in the Fourth Industrial Revolution may well leave out large portions of society. Societies and companies are confronted with a pressure to adapt, so that they cannot evade the debate on this issue.

Case in Point: BPN

The Business Professionals Network (BPN) is a charitable organization that promotes small business development in developing countries. It builds a bridge between the developed world and developing countries by transferring sound business management practices in order to strengthen the long-term future and competitiveness of small and medium sized companies in Asia, Africa and South America. It is an effective, high cost but high reward venture paying off in multiple ways: when people find a career perspective in their home country, they become more settled and secure. Strongly, locally rooted companies are important socioeconomic pillars. Additionally, they are more crisis resistant and willing to operate ecologically and responsibly. The willingness to migrate in transition countries is decreased and leads to a gradual, collective improvement. Or in the words of Maimonides, scholar and philosopher: *"Give a man a fish and you feed him for a day; teach a man to fish and you feed him for a lifetime."*

In many ways, the BPN development program is unique. The organization offers selected and participating entrepreneurs a range of structured education and coaching based programs. Over a period of two to four years, entrepreneurs are taken on through courses in business fundamentals such as accounting, planning, marketing, leadership development etc. The program has a modular structure and is individually tailored to the participants. BPN works with the entrepreneur on a value-based, practical basis and according to transparent accounting principles.

To put this theory in action, look at the following example in Rwanda: when carpenter Emil met us and we jointly decided to include him in the BPN program, his company employed four people. During the first two years, he applied to BPN for a loan for his machinery – specifically a wood drying plant. This was granted after a detailed investigation. Emil paid the loan back over a period of four years. Without exception, Emil attended every seminar that BPN offered and as a result, developed into a capable and responsible entrepreneur. BPN donor, by sponsoring a company, enabled him to participate in the BPN program and to ensure that he was assisted and guided during that period. Emil's carpentry grew steadily and developed splendidly. Today, his company employs 28 people and provides stability for them and their families. This is true help for self-help!

The BPN Foundation has been pursuing its mission to support talented entrepreneurs in building small and medium-sized companies in developing countries for over 20 years. Thousands of entrepreneurs and families are living a better life. This would not be possible without the understanding and commitment of an increasing number of people who see Purpose transformation not just as next level of obtaining competitive advantage for themselves in the 21st century, but a way to do good and give back also.

The *Blue Genie* Effect

"We have a lamp inside us.
The oil of that lamp is our breathing,
our steps, and our peaceful smile.
Our practice is to light up the lamp."

Thich Nhat Hanh
Zen Master

Personalized technology is the disrupting force of marketing. As it drives and empowers the consumer, it influences (purchase) behavior, channels of choice and budgets. It is therefore no surprise that the 'technology factor' within the overall marketing expenditure has soared over the past decade – with no end in sight.

An exponentially growing tendency in the world of commerce is to blend advanced media technologies with customer-centricity. Billions of dollars are being invested in consumer behavior research including big data and analytics, in-depth studies of the unconscious (neuroscience, psychoanalysis, behavioral economics, etc.), psychographics and so on. All of which will have paramount implications for the future of marketing. The direction in which the *why* question within consumer research is headed is leading us to a peculiar stage in the brand–client relationship. The consumer has more choice than ever, and the brand wants to know more than anything who the consumer is and what he or she really wants. More importantly, brands want to know why the consumer prefers their brand or product to their competitors. In many ways, it is about predicting what consumers want before they know they want it. It is also about offering them something better than anything they could ever wish for.

So, then the future role of marketing is metaphorically similar to the role of the *Blue Genie* from oriental folklore. All the Genie cares about is being your best friend and he is dying to figure out what it is he could do for you to make that happen. It is not that your wish is his command. No, customer-centricity is not just about serving, glorifying or loving the consumer. It is about creating meaningful bonds by crafting a product or experience that exceeds expectations and generates advocacy, lasting impressions and loyalty.

Again, it is the luxury sector that offers us excellent insights into the inner workings of how to achieve great customer appreciation. Paradoxically, most luxury brands probably invest the least in Big Data analytics and yet, they are closer to understanding how to get customers to rub the lamp than any other sector. Banks, for instance, invest a ton in marketing compared to luxury brands, spreading ads in which they merely claim to be customer-centric although they are miles away from being a *Blue Genie*. A few years ago, NatWest (a subsidiary of the Royal Bank of Scotland) ran a huge multimillion-dollar advertising campaign across the UK under the promising name of 'helpful banking.' The ads literally claimed that, "We have listened to thousands of people" and "That's why we are now open on Saturdays." This was certainly attractive to people working during the week. Sadly, only 675 out of the 1552 NatWest branches across the country actually opened on Saturdays.[75] In other words, two-thirds of the bank's clientele were excited about the offer and potentially visited a branch on Saturday only to learn that the campaign was a disappointing half-truth. Naturally, the NatWest brand suffered a loss of trust. As long as banks and other sectors continue to look at brand management as a pure enabler of more short-term sales, they will never become a *Blue Genie*.

It is no wonder that the coming generation of consumers trusts luxury brands, boutique companies, but equally tech companies such as Google, Amazon etc. more than they trust the establishment of large corporate brands. Google is the perfect example of a tech company that does everything it can to reach the most personalized level of organizing and presenting information to those who seek it. The first version of Google was literally the same for everyone. Today, every one of us has a personalized Google search algorithm of our own in addition to a global and local one. With each use, recommendations get better and more accurate. In Google's case, the *Blue Genie* effect occurs when the search engine pre-recognizes what you are searching for and provides top results fulfilling your wishes before you've made them. Google's reason for being? To organize the world's information and make it universally accessible and useful.[76]

Meta-personalization, humanization and rationalization are among the key macro-themes of the future. Understanding and adopting truly customer-centric approaches to value creation will result in better products, services, experiences and overall humanize touch points between brands and consumers, rubbing the lamp in order to finally embellish what is within. Being stuck inside the lamp for thousands of years gave the Genie a crick in the neck. The time has come to let it out.

Heroes, Giants, Gods

*"If I have seen further it is by standing
on the shoulders of giants."*

Sir Isaac Newton
Physicist and Mathematician

Many of the ancient belief systems of humankind were based on personifying the great forces of nature. These forces became heroes – giants, mythological gods, angels, demigods, etc. Humanity and society as we know it today went through great shifts such as the Enlightenment and the Industrial Revolution, perhaps due to our human need to personify.

Aspiring to have infinite wisdom, as the mythological gods had, was perhaps what motivated us to create the internet – a technological space that provides infinite information anytime and anywhere. We are not claiming that the father of the internet, Tim Berners-Lee was 'led by the gods,' but gaining immediate access to knowledge accumulated over thousands of years is one of those achievements that has given us a god-like ability. Indeed, the internet is said to have a lot in common with the human brain, for example. The human brain and man's desire to emulate it inspire much of today's research in cognitive computing. By no means are we gods, but the mythological heroes our ancestors imagined have served as a source of guidance in our attempts to extend human capabilities. Philosophers dreaming about immortality have encouraged us to find ways to extend our lives. Today, we live longer lives and witness more events and phenomena in one lifetime than any generation before us. Future generations will live twice as long as today's average lifespan and see even more throughout their lives. They will live to be much wiser, as they will be around long enough to recognize life's patterns.

Yet our well of inspiration is not limited to ancient mythological gods. Modern generations create heroes, too: James Bond, Superman, Don Draper, the X-Men, Steve Jobs, Nikola Tesla, etc. But what makes some heroes more influential than others? What kind of heroes should a brand associate itself with?

Let us contemplate three types of heroes:

Type 1: Fictional heroes with superhuman qualities (e.g., Superman)
Type 2: Semi-fictional heroes inspired by real world individuals
(e.g., James Bond, Don Draper)
Type 3: Heroes in our society doing extraordinary things
(e.g., Nikola Tesla, Leonardo da Vinci, etc.)

Consumers know that they can never be Type 1 heroes. Still, they can take on certain characteristics of one. Heroes and giants never fail; they are aspirational and have meaningful values that transcend society.

Engaging in multimillion-dollar deals with famous celebrities of mainstream culture as opposed to fictional heroes can be very risky. In fact, many luxury brands avoid working with celebrities in their brand management altogether. Aston Martin, for instance, refuses to hire anyone famous. A Type 2 hero like James Bond, however, is still a fictional character with fictitious human flaws and therefore, poses little to no risk. The key is figuring out which hero possesses those characteristics that best fit with your brand and can address your target audience without the risk of causing reputational damage.

The ancient Greeks anthropomorphized the great forces of nature. Zeus was depicted as a bearded old man with a strong fit body. Poseidon, the god of drought, flood, sea and earthquakes was also portrayed as a human being along with many other deities. You may find it amusing that they believed in such gods, but if you look at modern brand communications strategies you will notice that we have the same inclination to personify things. However, instead of attributing human qualities to the forces of nature, human beings now embody brands. As an instructive case study, let's take Dos Equis. It used to be an indistinct beer brand until it became the sixth largest imported beer sold in the USA.[77] When imported beer sales dropped 11%, Dos Equis sales rose more than 17%.[78] The turning point came about when The Most Interesting Man emerged. This bon vivant was the ultimate personification of the Dos Equis brand – a creation that ended up taking the product to another level. To be clear, this is not at all a success story of massive advertising. Rather, it is a result caused by the careful positioning of a Type 2 hero. It is a case of outthinking the competition, which is not the same as buying vast amounts of ad space to saturate the market. An even more nostalgic example is, of course, The Marlboro Man. While consumers may have a hard time identifying with tobacco wrapped in paper, they can easily sympathize with a masculine cowboy riding into the sunset.

What role do the heroes, giants and gods play for Purpose-oriented brands and individuals? There is a particular role that non-fictional giants and heroes (Type 3) play in brand management, organizational culture and entrepreneurship. Type 3 figures set the example and share their unconventional paths to success with the world. They are masters at setting new precedents. People don't do what their leaders say; they do what their leaders do. The 12th-century French philosopher Bernard of Chartres wrote that we [the Moderns] are like dwarfs perched on the shoulders of giants [the Ancients], and thus we are able to see much more and much farther. This is not at all because of our acute sight or the stature of our bodies, but because we are carried high and elevated by the magnitude of the giants. In his letter to the English polymath Robert Hooke, Sir Isaac Newton wrote the famous words: "If I have seen further it is by standing on the shoulders of giants." The heroes and giants of yesterday guide the heroes and giants of today and tomorrow.

In the case of luxury brands, the founder is most often the giant on whose shoulders later generations stand on. This is certainly true of Thierry Hermès, founder of Hermès; Louis- François Cartier, founder of Cartier; Peter Carl

Fabergé who created Fabergé; Abraham-Louis Breguet the innovator of the Breguet tourbillon, Antoni Patek and Adrien Philippe who founded Patek Philippe and so on. These founders were not mythological gods but creators of worlds. One of HSBC's ads targeted at small businesses, entrepreneurs and startup founders takes an interesting angle: "Founders are just people who found something they love. It is never just business." The minds behind luxury brands have something in common: they leave traces and marks in history and in the memories of descendants. Founders are by no means superhuman; they are human beings like the rest of us. It is just that they have found their core Purpose in life.

Transformation of Value Chains

"Lots of companies don't succeed over time.
What do they fundamentally do wrong?
They usually miss the future."

Larry Page
Co-Founder and former CEO, Google

Dr Clotaire Rapaille, market researcher and anthropologist, who conducts research on the cultural unconscious, explained that after half a century of research he discovered something fundamentally different from all his previous archetypal findings. He found that Generation Y represents a global generation with a universal set of values, regardless of their culture, ethnicity or nationality. We can reason that this is partly due to the existence of a supreme network, a topic we shall address in the next chapter. The volume, the speed and the intensity of connectivity, enabled through fast bandwidth and low-cost access points, is increasing drastically. As a consequence, we are witnessing the rise of platforms, increasing transparency and the elimination of the middlemen. Airbnb, Uber and others are prime examples of how the digital revolution creates a disruptive force and unleashes unforeseen challenges.

Generation Y needs to see and believe the brands' Know-Why. This generation serves as a proxy for what we believe is only the beginning of much more value-chain disruption to come. Post-millennial generations will innately look for Purpose-led brands. Their expectations represent a new era of competitive risks for traditionally geared companies. As transparency increases, consumers have the power to 'see through' brands as they look behind the creation of products for integrity and real, honest social responsibility. This means that brands will more than ever need to control not only their own operations, but also those of their entire supply chain. Consumers can and will eliminate corporations that don't behave well and back those exemplary organizations that demonstrate absolute integrity in everything they deliver. A Gallup survey on Purpose found that "when promise and behavior are in sync and customers are aligned with a brand promise, they give that brand twice as much share of wallet (47%) as customers who aren't aligned with that same brand (23%)."[79] Essentially, brands that fail to match what they say with what they do won't win.

Hermès, a French luxury brand, found its Purpose in 'Keeping Craftsmanship Alive.'[80] While Hermès is in many ways a true Purpose-driven brand, the company failed to control its supply chain, which eventually led to an unexpected crisis in 2015. All it took was a short clip posted on YouTube going viral. The video showed the cruel slaughtering of crocodiles at a Texan animal farm used for the production of Hermès' handbags. Actress and namesake Jane Birkin (as in 'Hermès Birkin Bag, going anywhere from a few thousand dollars to $100,000+) posted on Twitter that 'Hermès remove her name from the Birkin bag with immediate effect[81] This worsened the impact of the scandal, damaged brand perception and identity at a speed the company was hardly able to keep up with. Clearly, articulating a well-crafted Purpose is not enough. Purpose needs to be lived internally and throughout the value chain in order to uphold the level of integrity today's consumers demand.

The tectonic shift towards digitalization and transparency are pushing consumers to look at corporate integrity. It is an indication that our beliefs and value systems are going through a metamorphosis. The consumers' opinion is a powerful disruptive force to be reckoned with, changing the very idea of commercial competition. Technological paradigm shifts are reshaping the media, marketing and consumer electronics industries, but also the finance sector. In fact, cyber finance has become one of the most essential components of the entire economic system.

One of the earliest shifts in finance occurred when precious metals were replaced with promissory notes, eliminating the correlation between the value of currencies and the scarcity of gold. The age of digitalization has put the currency system through another transition, whereby no physical element is left to represent value. Everything is made of 1s and 0s. Only a small percentage of all the money in the world exists as physical cash or as gold. Such terms as online banking, e-finance, fin-tech, mobile banking and so on have become a daily part of our language. It is not incidental that Michael Lewis's book entitled *Flash Boys* remained number one on the *New York Times* bestsellers list for weeks. His book essentially examines how the speed of data creates competitive advantage in high- frequency trading. In addition to the speed of data, the role of crypto currency is also becoming more important. Bitcoin is one of the early indicators of this. According to MarketWatch, a US$1000 investment in Bitcoin in 2010 would be worth about US$35 million today.[82] Bitcoin operates on blockchain technology, a decentralized and distributed digital ledger that records and validates transactions across thousands of independent computers. The upside? Records in the shared ledger cannot be modified retroactively without the alteration of all subsequent blocks and the collusion of the network – essentially, they are almost impossible to hack. In theory, this means we no longer need to put our trust into banks to authorize monetary transactions. Indeed, the fundamental proposition upon which banking is built is at stake.

However, value chain disruption goes a lot further. Blockchain is an 'open source' or communal technology, for which no usage fees, royalties or other monetary compensation is due. Whilst a bank charges high fees for an international money transfer, let's say, blockchain technology enables the same transfer at practically zero cost. In short, blockchain has the potential to be a truly powerful disruptive force: a network within the financial system can outweigh the functions of an individual bank simply for the fact that it can provide more secure and personalized services to clients at near-zero cost.

However, what makes blockchain technology truly fascinating is that it is by far not limited to currency or financial transactions. Blockchain can provide the trust layer where there is a potential trust issue, providing the glue and transparency in value chains to address issues related to sustainability, transparency and privacy. For instance, the global luxury conglomerate

LVMH has developed a blockchain platform called Aura through which it is possible to track luxury goods' supply chains to prove their authenticity or verify that they were manufactured by the original source.[83] Lamborghini too is planning to implement blockchain in supply chain operations.[84] Whilst it's only the beginning, key improvements in this area indicate that blockchain's mainstream adoption is on its way.

Value chain transformation is without a doubt redefining business and the nature of competition. As Buckminster Fuller explained, there is almost nothing about a caterpillar that tells you it's going to be a butterfly. From our perspective, and taking into account the angles examined so far, we can only conclude that a collective movement is underway to return to an Economy of Qualities, where trust is no longer measured by what you say or promise, but by what you actually do, how you demonstrate it and how others judge you for it.

Case in Point: Airbnb

Embedding Purpose within a disruptive business model.

Airbnb is a company run and founded by a millennial generation who saw an opportunity in the simplicity of offering people a cheaper alternative to booking accommodation at hotels. A sound business idea that had a nice side effect: the fun of staying at someone else's place for an authentic cultural experience away from home.

Airbnb offers an interesting perspective to the extent that it recognized the power of Purpose and embedded it early on in its existence. A short analysis of Airbnb's brand video on the company's identity[85] reveals the essence of the company's inner Purpose: 'To Belong.' The idea of belonging implies becoming part of a specific community, which takes Airbnb's proposition way beyond the transactional ease of finding a place to stay at a lower cost. It now also stands for belonging when in a foreign place and culture.

A Swiss traveling to Japan, for instance, can feel more like a local staying in a Kyoto residential apartment, even if it's just for a few days. The same is true for the other end of the value chain – people offering their places on Airbnb also 'belong' in the sense that they engage with guests and enrich their visit by offering insider tips. It goes without saying that 'to belong' also serves as an inner Purpose with which staff and wider stakeholders can identify.

We see more and more companies coming to the realization that properly embedding Purpose into the core of their business model is a necessity, especially startups and young companies. Some examples include Sourcemap, EveryMove and BetterDoctor. Many large-sized firms, on the other hand, are late in recognizing the indispensable nature of Purpose. It requires a certain mindset, willingness and the ability to see how influential and enabling Purpose can be. Tesla, for instance, has discovered its Purpose as well: 'Accelerating the transition to electric mobility.' The question is – is it possible to retrofit a Purpose to an organization? For young organizations with a brand culture in the making, this is a relatively straightforward exercise. It is much harder to integrate Purpose thinking inside out into established global corporations because Purpose sits at the very core of an organization's culture. Still it is not entirely impossible. There is an increasing number of companies global in nature and of considerable size that do run on Purpose; Apple, Google, Ernst & Young, HBR, to name a few. And the network is expanding.

The Supreme Network

"Learn how to see.
Realize that everything connects to everything else."

Leonardo da Vinci
Italian Polymath

Omni-integration is the future, although the concept of connecting everything with everything is not at all new. For millennials, great thinkers from religion, art and science to philosophy have contemplated it. The idea that 'all being connected to all' is somehow linked with 'universal truth' has been a part of the dialogue among Zen Buddhists and Sufi philosophers, for instance. The idea of omni-connection holds that what is alike attracts what is alike, and all is alike on our planet. Therefore, all is connected. The forests on our planet are like the hair on our heads. The rocks and stones are like our skull and bones. The rivers are designed like our nerves and veins. The chaotic cities are like the neural circuitry in our brains.

One of the biggest advances of humanity is without a doubt the invention and continuous perfection of massive communication networks. From runners and carrier pigeons to telegraph, radio, phone and TV, to the interactive nature of smartphones and the Internet of Things. And beyond. However, raising the quantity of connections doesn't proportionally raise the quality of connections. Where does the opportunity lie in a world where the speed, the quantity and intensity of connectivity keeps expanding exponentially? Connection quality is what will determine real value in the future. New economies of quality will become part of a larger cultural shift towards an inner paradigm of authenticity, meaning and sincerity as an antidote to the twentieth century phenomenon of mass-producing more of the same. It is not about how many connections one has, but rather how the quality of those connections interrelates. Similarly, it is not about the number of brand associations that exist in the minds of consumers, but about the quality of those associations. Creating value, then, requires maximizing the quality (not quantity) of messages in order to build stronger bridges between brands and individuals.

If connectedness is already a big theme today, it is nothing compared to what is yet to come. Internet.org, a large-scale initiative led by Facebook, is bringing together technology leaders, nonprofits and local communities to provide internet access to those who are not yet connected. Virgin Group founder, Sir Richard Branson, shared a similar vision at a World Economic Forum: "We [Virgin Galactic] are planning to put up an array of satellites, nearly 1500 from day one and up to 3000 satellites over a span of time." Communities in need will be able to install small satellite dishes on the rooftops of homes, schools, and universities to get connected. Google has also launched an R&D project called Loon for Everyone. Its mission is to provide internet access with high-altitude balloons that sail through the stratosphere and create an aerial wireless network. SpaceX, founded by Elon Musk, raised $1 billion in funding to provide internet access to rural, remote and underserved regions around the globe. The plan calls for launching a constellation of 4,000 small and inexpensive satellites that would beam high-speed internet signals to all parts of the globe, including its most remote regions. According to Musk, the effort "would be like rebuilding the internet in space."[86]

As of 2019, roughly 4.5 billion people, or about 58% of the world's population, have internet access, the large majority of whom are in Asia.[87] There is little doubt that in the near future, even more people will be connected to even more people. More people will be connected to more information, and the Internet of Things (IoT) will begin to connect all things to other things. From the perspective of agriculture for instance, farmers will have access to better weather data, which can improve their profitability. Healthcare will benefit from newly found possibilities in the form of closed-loop insulin delivery, activity trackers during cancer treatment, self-testing devices that will help patients stay within their therapeutic range and lower the risk of stroke or bleeding and so on. The opportunities IoT offers are quite literally endless and mark a new era in how we will live in the future.

But connectedness is progressively going beyond the 'net' and reaching deeper than a mere exchange of information. In a world that is gradually digitized, the value of physical connections will become a crucial antidote. The Aston Martin key is an illustrative example of the value of touch. To roar up a powerful V8 or V12 Aston Martin engine, you don't need a 'key'; you need what the company calls an Emotional Control Unit (ECU). Although Aston Martin has the technology and capacity to design a car with keyless ignition, the brand keeps it as an integral part of the customer experience. The key has been transformed into a symbol of prestige in a time when even your average Ford Fiesta offers keyless ignition. It is not an automatic connection, but a manual one, whereby the Emotional Control Unit connects you to something much larger than the car. As Friedrich Nietzsche writes in his book *Thus Spoke Zarathustra*: "All anew, all eternal, all enlinked, enlaced and enamored. Oh, then did ye LOVE the world." Nietzsche refers to a world in which all is not only interconnected, but it is also united in an ultimate supreme network.

Connectedness to such an extreme degree is perhaps difficult to grasp today, as the internet has almost become a biological organism in itself, a continually evolving brain, if you will. Artificial Intelligence (AI) is taking on thoughts through cognitive computing, and Virtual Reality (VR) gradually replicates feelings and thus emotions. Skeptics already forewarn of the coming 'singularity' – i.e. a state in which technology functions as 'one' and will have the power to outsmart us humble human beings. But let's not get ahead of ourselves. Perhaps a better metaphor to help us apprehend the interconnectedness of the future is the neural networks of our brains. It is worth reminding ourselves that the Web is nothing (yet) compared to the network in our brains in terms of speed and complexity. When we use our brains to help us understand a difficult concept, we are actually doing what networks do, namely making associations, connecting, linking, contacting and so on. Metaphors are integral elements of human language, and human language works as a network-like system of codes, meanings, and symbols. The bottom line is that when we are unable to explain something complex, metaphors help us out. By association we connect a concept or a thought to something similar to simplify that concept and make it more comprehensible. In reaching higher levels of connectedness, the human understanding of universal truth will advance at an unprecedented speed. Our networks will begin to match those of our neural system where digital bonds between things, people and information networks will be like the air we breathe – invisible and essential.

Connecting everything also means cutting out the middle and giving rise to platforms that enable and facilitate exchange of economic value without the necessity to hold, store or ship tangible goods, for instance. Tom Goodwin, Senior VP of Strategy and Innovation at Havas Media, famously summarized the transformational nature of today's world, saying: "Uber, the world's largest taxi company, owns no vehicles. Facebook, the world's most popular media owner, creates no content. Alibaba, the most valuable retailer, has no inventory. And Airbnb, the world's largest accommodation provider, owns no real estate. Something interesting is happening."

It is important to understand that connections will not only intensify, but the volume and number of channels will continue to grow exponentially, too. There will be more information, but also new sources of information. Consequently, both large and small corporations must be conscious of the fact that increased connectivity and speed will not only make transparency more relevant than ever, but it will also intensify interdependence. Genuine transparency in business will become the macro-theme of future commerce. Already today, consumers can pull their phones out of their pockets and with a few taps compare not just prices and service quality, but also brand reputation. They can check if you are paying your employees enough or if your supply chain is sustainable. The fundamentals of trade have begun to move beyond monetary transaction.

In such an environment, the function of a *Guiding Purpose Strategy* is essential for anyone intending to stay ahead of the curve. As we enter this new epoch of omni-integration, the ability to find and clarify an overarching Purpose will offer a key to success. Putting Purpose at the core of business strategy will connect employees, suppliers and customers in unprecedented ways. Purpose will constitute the tree of life, rather than industry expertise, and it will enable those who touch it to connect with an entire ecosystem of the organization – the supreme network.

In an opinion economy driven by a supreme network, building authenticity, honesty and integrity into your value chain is not only critical for success, but it is a question of survival. If these core values aren't integral components of your internal operations, consumers will 'see' this and switch to a brand that satisfies their modern demands. Consumers will simply tune you out. The transformational powers at work here cannot be underestimated.

Slow Death

*"The greatest trick the devil ever pulled
was convincing the world he didn't exist."*

Verbal
from *The Usual Suspects*

Today century-old companies can disappear within a matter of months if they blatantly disrespect the trust consumers have put in them. Marginal price differences are becoming an insignificant aspect for customers when choosing one product over another, especially when the integrity of value systems is at stake. It is critical to recall that for the first time ever, an entire generation with common value denominators are emerging. The Purpose agenda will, in a sense, force a Darwinian lens over brands and businesses. The strongest and fittest will survive.

We claim that companies not implementing a *Guiding Purpose Strategy* will likely be facing a slow death. Perhaps this rather cruel frog experiment will help exemplify what we mean: If one puts a frog into heated water, the frog will jump out to survive. However, if the water is heated gradually, the frog dies a slow death. It isn't aware of the danger, so it doesn't bother to respond to the changing environment.

There are still many companies unaware that the world of commerce is in transition. We've already seen over 50% of the Fortune 500 companies disappearing since the year 2000[88] – suffering through a progression we call slow death. Mainly hit by 'digital disruption,' these are companies that also ignore the Purpose component and ultimately meet their demise, often to their surprise.

The 'too big to fail' expression has lost its meaning and relevance. Do you remember Enron, PanAm, Blockbuster, Compaq and Eastern Airlines?[89] This is just to name a few large corporations that were great at crafting long-winded and lofty mission statements but failed to clearly define their core Purpose. These companies were once in the top five within their sectors.

Organizations that died like our frog weren't aware of what was happening to them. The greatest trick the grim reaper ever pulled was to convince global corporations that he doesn't exist. Death doesn't send you a WhatsApp or a Facebook message to tell you that your company or indeed, your entire industry has been chosen. It silently and perpetually sneaks up on you. The warning signs are scarce and hard to spot, but they are there if you are willing to face them. The most important question is often ignored simply because it is human nature to live in denial: is my brand or my company on the road to death?

If we take into account the democratization of knowledge today, we realize that Know-How is becoming insufficient. If we further bear in mind that decentralization is at work both in business and global politics, we can begin to grasp that simply owning the biggest market share isn't enough. There is plenty of evidence already that companies with a clear Purpose outperform those that lack one. Sheth, Wolfe and Sisodia explain how world-class companies profit from passion and Purpose. They demonstrate how Purpose led companies outperform the market by a 9:1 ratio over a ten-year period.[90]

In order to define strategy, the Know-How is not enough anymore because today the Know-How needs to be complemented with the know-where and the most vital of it all: the Know-Why.

On Purpose

Why do you do what you do?

"When a brand combines Purpose with passion,
the powerful impact it creates ripples,
serving to help create a better world."

Dr Dimitrios Tsivrikos
Contributing Author, University College London
Consumer and Business Psychologist

Humans strive for a Purpose in life, a sense of being that is bigger than themselves. Equally, brands strive for a higher reason to exist, in addition to generating an economic return. Brands encapsulate this in their value systems, what they stand for, and how they aim to improve their customers' lives through their products and services, as well as changing the world for the better. Brands are able to use their Purpose to distinguish themselves from the rest of the industry and knowing the deeper Purpose of a company's existence lays the foundation on which to build every experience. One famous example of a successful Purpose-driven brand is Dove who create advertisements centered around body positivity and helping consumers create a healthy relationship with beauty products, reflecting their own personal care product line.

The development of brand Purpose is one of the most important features that an up-and-coming business needs to accomplish, however, it's a task that often gets overlooked. While three out of four brands outline their Purpose to make a positive impact on society, nowhere near this many companies can actually demonstrate how this Purpose is shown through their work[91]. Most companies fall into one of three categories with respect to Purpose: prioritizers, companies that have a clearly articulated and understood Purpose (39%); developers, companies that have not established a clear Purpose but are working towards developing one (48%); and laggards, companies which have not developed a Purpose (13%).[92] Prioritizing companies demonstrate higher performance levels than developing or laggard companies across a number of business activities. So how do successful companies develop their brand Purpose?

The biggest companies think broadly, looking to see what they are hoping to change in the world, not just in their specific industry or company, and how they will work continuously to fulfil this Purpose. The Golden Circle by Simon Sinek perfectly illustrates how companies cultivate Purpose. The circle represents: WHAT, HOW and WHY[93]. Every organization knows WHAT they do – the products they sell or services they offer. Some organizations know HOW they do it – the characteristics which set their products apart from others. Very few organizations know WHY they do what they do. A famous example of this is Apple. Instead of following the standard marketing technique of communicating what they do and how they are different, Apple begins by communicating its Purpose to empower creative exploration and self-expression.

Brand Purpose is becoming even more salient; thus, companies must awaken to the changing customer market. This trend is being spearheaded by younger generations (millennials and Generation Z) who have been shown to buy in line with their beliefs more than previous generations, with 65% of the population now following this way of purchasing[94]. The Edelman survey also found that, once consumers have found a brand that aligns with their beliefs, they are more willing to stay loyal to and advocate for the brand in question. Beyond just attracting consumers, the Purposes these brands stand for are also important in recruiting and retaining employees with current issues such as #MeToo, immigration, and diversity as examples of those that young employees expect their companies to stand up for, or at least engage with. Behavioral psychologists refer to this phenomenon as attempts to minimize cognitive dissonance, potential inconsistencies in consumers' thoughts and behavioral decisions. Loyal customers and employees aren't the only benefits gained through having a Purpose. With Purpose comes profit. EY recently published the results of a three-year-old study, finding that prioritizers faced a 58% growth compared to 42% and 50% of laggards and developers.[95] Brands are now omnipotent, attracting ever more followers. It is often not even too far-fetched to compare follow-ship to religious cults and congregations. Power brands such as Supreme for instance can command messages at unprecedented levels of influence. A fine example of a brand which has established an almost religious following, Coca-Cola, takes the lead. Experiencing happiness is their mantra, capturing our attention throughout the year with joyful imagery from cool refreshments in the summer, to Santa Claus in the winter. Their entire business works to instill happiness in every can and every home around the world.

Without Purpose companies can suffer, as companies which do not align with customers beliefs pay the price. There is also still an element of distrust surrounding advertisements, with almost 70% of consumers reporting distrust in them, and 42% distrusting brands as a whole[96]. The necessity for brands to act upon their promises is paramount, with 58% of adults reporting distrust in brands until they have proven that they are sticking to their word[97]. Based on this distrust, consumers are not afraid to boycott brands when they do not stand up for social issues. Globally, customer dissatisfaction has led to 90% of consumers being willing to boycott if they learned of a company's irresponsible business practices[98]. Companies that don't communicate their Purpose effectively are also in danger of being boycotted. Take Mastercard for example, who created an advert during the UEFA Champions League stating that they would give 10,000 children a meal every time Lionel Messi or Neymar Jr scored a goal. At first look it's not a bad idea, but then you ask, well, if they have the resources to give away these meals, why are they waiting for an overpaid footballer to do his job before they help these children?

Overall, it seems that brand Purpose is an important feature for the initial mission of attracting and retaining consumers, and perhaps now employees as well. Consumers have expectations of the brands they choose to stand up for important issues societal issues. Ultimately, in this constantly changing world, Purpose-driven companies are the ones that remain on top. They attract the best minds, have the most passionate consumers, achieve success and change the world. When a brand combines Purpose with passion, the powerful impact it creates ripples, serving to help create a better world.

Essence and Appearance

"Clients will always remember a negative experience
no matter how many positive moments have been shared."

Andrea Soriani
Head of Marketing
Maserati North America

In Greek philosophy, the concept of 'essence' is of particular interest. Aristotle originated it and linked the notion of essence to the idea of *definition*, which is quite a useful vehicle for reaching pragmatic goals. In fact, the concept of 'real essence' has been at the center of much of the philosophical debate since the 17th century. Metaphysically – that which is beyond physics – to ask what the essence of something is, is akin to asking what that something really is, fundamentally, what it does and why it exists.

There is a certain kind of tension in any child's life as he or she grows and learns about the world. Much of this tension is directly or indirectly related to essence and appearance. As the years go by and the child grows, certain events in life demonstrate how things are not always what they appear to be. Likewise, the essence of an appearance may be good. All that glitters is not gold: not everything that looks precious or true turns out to be so. This tension between appearance and essence plays a delicate role in business as

119

well. From our perspective, whether it is associated with an entrepreneur, an organization, a brand or even an individual, essence should not be confused with identity or soul. Essence defines the inner self, while identity is the appearance. Without essence, identity can be unstable, fragile, unreliable, uncertain and fleeting. We are not suggesting that identity or appearance is less important. Rather, we want to stress the fact that the function of 'essence' cannot be overemphasized.

Business literature on brand management often discusses the notion of 'brand essence', but there are still too few executives who truly grasp the meaning of it. This is simply because most brand managers around the world are disproportionately focused on 'brand appearance' and pay the crucial role of brand essence too little attention. Rumi, the 13th-century poet, jurist and Sufi mystic, said: "Either appear as you are or be as you appear." In the context of 21st-century brand management, we translate Rumi's great words to mean that it is time for companies to synchronize appearance with essence.

A survey conducted by the Co-Operative Bank found that over a three-year period business that projected themselves as having a strong ethical orientation increased their market share by 30%.[99] Traditional ways of doing business allowed space for cheap tricks, but the days of shallow marketing are over. In other words, marketing is embarking on a new era in which outer appearance must be in sync with the real inner essence of the value proposition, the firm, or the individual.

So, how do we synchronize appearance with essence? First of all, it is necessary to keep the descriptive close to the prescriptive. In short, the worlds of 'what it should be' and 'what it is' must not exist too far from each other. The gap must be closed.

The Hidden P's of Marketing

"There is something behind the throne greater than the king himself."

Sir William Pitt
1st Earl of Chatham and British Statesman

The famous 4 P's of marketing, as defined by marketing guru Philip Kotter, are no longer enough to define our marketplace. Product, Price, Place and Promotion are still essential in defining a value proposition and answering questions such as how much to charge, where and how to sell and how to win customers. While the classic P's help us define our marketing mix, they are also more than half a century old. They were very relevant helping brand builders and marketers navigate through the 20th century, but the world and its consumers have most definitely moved on.

Given our discussion so far, we believe the marketing mix should be expanded by three additional P's: (P)hysical environment, (P)eople and (P)rocess. Physical environment, because we can no longer build propositions in isolation of their impact without considering the greater agenda of interdependencies. People, because we live in an era of radical transparency where opinions form a new currency. And finally Process, because value chain disruption is systemic.

More importantly, however, are the Hidden P's of Marketing: Passion, Perseverance and Purpose. "He who perseveres is a man of Purpose." – said Lao Tzu. These are perhaps the most essential P's, enriching the creation of a perfect marketing mix. Passion is needed to excite and rally people to create. Perseverance is seeing actions, plans and bold ideas through. And Purpose is what holds everything and everyone together. These three P's are often hard to spot because they reside in the inner world of an individual or an internal culture of an organization. They are less tangible than the creation of a new product, brand or marketing mix. Without these three hidden P's, all the others hardly have a chance of optimizing Return- On-Investment (ROI) in the long run.

There is a strong relationship between Purpose and Passion. A person who has found his or her Purpose can't help but show contagious enthusiasm and commitment to that which makes him or her happy. Not every passionate person has found Purpose, but those who have, innately inject passion into whatever matters to them. As John Calvin Maxwell explains in his work on leadership: "People don't care how much you know until they know how much you care."

If college students came across more teachers and professors who were passionate about their fields, they may get curious about a particular field themselves and start to develop a passion for it. Understanding and mastering the hidden P's of marketing requires us to be at least familiar with the language of Purpose and the contagiousness of passion. Otherwise, your chances of eloquently leveraging passion and perseverance will be slim. Remember the universal law of social interaction? Only boring people are bored and only interested people are interesting.

While Purpose with a capital P is not always readily visible to the naked eye, it manifests all around us. As Ralph Waldo Emerson put it, "Good luck is another name for tenacity of Purpose." Research shows that Purpose-driven companies in the S&P 500 boast returns of 1025% over a ten-year period, compared to just 122% of the rest.[100] We tend to notice the extraordinary creations that stem from Purpose without giving it sufficient credit. Not all creation is shaped by one's Purpose and not all creation is meaningful. However, those creations that live long lifecycles withstanding the test of time are those brought to fruition by a deep, inner Purpose.

The Shaman and the Meaningful Brand

"The very meaninglessness of life forces man to create his own meaning."

Stanley Kubrick
American Film Director and Editor

When our ancestors first became conscious of their existence a new immortal need was born – the need to make meaning. Leading a meaningless life creates a demand for an agent, a leader who could make meaning out of all things in daily life, including nature and humanity itself. When conducting ethnographic fieldwork, we had the opportunity to meet with Kara-ool Tulushevich Dopchun-ool, the Supreme Shaman of the Republic of Tuva, to discuss the inner workings of Shamanism. The Siberians coined the term 'shaman.' Traditional Turkic Shamanism is one of the oldest, if not the first, proxy to creating a belief system and spreading knowledge in the pre-civilization and pre-religion era. The shaman was the one who presented value systems and gave meaningful explanations about the future, teaching that the source of it all was a deep Purpose hidden within each individual.

We've come a long way since the birth of consciousness, but our collective craving for meaning has not ceased. In fact, it has only increased. The relevance of an overarching Purpose in life is even stronger today because we now understand that it is the source from which satisfaction is derived.

Our drive to find meaning and Purpose in life is what distinguishes us from animals. It is what got us out of the woods and onto the plains. The continuing evolution of man has sparked cultural progress and systems of values have emerged.

In his book called *The Ad Man and the Shaman*,[101] Ahmet Gungoren, a Turkish copywriter and cultural anthropologist, highlights the persistent presence of the human desire to find meaning. In prehistoric times, new belief systems and storytellers gained importance due to an urge to make sense of the surrounding world. The scientific revolution, for example, was the result of a deep human need to make sense of nature.

Coming back to business, we believe that there will be less and less room for meaningless brands, firms, products and services simply because it is in our human nature to seek meaning. If an enterprise lacks Purpose and fails to contribute to society in a meaningful way, its relevance will be put into question.

While there are plenty of marketing gurus, there are too few marketing shamans. But we can learn to be agents of meaning by comprehending that value comes from Purpose and that sustainable profitability is not achievable without it. The Shamanic question is: Are you and your organization ready to make the necessary paradigmatic shift and infuse your business with true, inner meaning?

The Guiding Purpose

"If we understood our cognitive limitations in the same way that we understand our physical limitations ... we could design a better world."

Dan Ariely
Professor of Behavioral Economics
Duke University

According to Peter Pearson, a marital and couples' psychologist, the Holy Grail of relationships is about finding a person who shares the same core values. As time goes by, chemical or physical attraction can fade, but shared values remain a solid fundament. One can negotiate one's interests, but deep values and, even more so, one's guiding Purpose is non-negotiable. Spending your life with those that share the same core values helps you live a fulfilling life.[102]

Bronnie Ware, an Australian nurse who spent several years working in palliative care, caring for patients in the last 12 weeks of their lives recorded the regrets of the dying.[103] She asked her terminally ill patients if they had any regrets and if they could go back in time, what they would do differently. The number one regret was not having the courage to live a life true to oneself. Realizing too late that you haven't followed your inner Purpose makes you feel that you've made an irreversible mistake. The same goes for brands and businesses, of course.

Many people in their eighties today are not able to look back at their lives and articulate a particular Purpose. They may have had unconscious ambitions and desires that drove them to achieve certain things, but they grew up in very different times, where life was about survival for most people. Neither did they have the luxury to invest time and effort in reflecting on the greater meaning to what they did, nor was it perceived as something vital to life by society at large.

Looking back at the first half of the 20th century, it becomes clear that it is easier today for young generations to live a life with an inner Purpose. According to a Gallup survey, 87% of today's teens think that their lives have an overall Purpose.[104] For some of the older generations, living life with an inner Purpose was not necessarily socially accepted. Ones choices in life were perceived as radical or rebellious if they did not fit within the social norms. Luckily times have changed. Now there is more choice than ever: women's rights and individual human rights have progressed, nations are less isolated, science, speech and commerce enjoy more freedom, knowledge and education can be developed and explored. The reasons to find Purpose in life are perhaps the same as they have always been, but we now have more liberty to pursue this quest. Today's challenge is more about weeding through the clutter of choice and information to find inner meaning. While it is more socially acceptable to embark on a search for Purpose in life, one must have the skills to pinpoint the needle in a haystack.

The same goes for companies and brands, too. When demand is driven by the economic value of making things faster and cheaper, a non-monetary reflection on values and Purpose seems senseless. The mantra has been to minimize cost and maximize (monetary) profit, so why bother connecting it to a larger, deeper, higher Purpose? The *why* question is missing in this very industrial mode of thinking. This is no surprise – it is hard to pause and gain consciousness of 'existence.'

As markets become even more competitive and cluttered, companies begin to recognize that clever market positioning alone will no longer be enough.

They needed to answer the *Why* question. Hence our view that Purpose will define the 'post-positioning' era. Boardroom discussions on Purpose finally ensue within those companies advanced enough to acknowledge the positive impact a well-articulated and embedded Purpose can have.

Perhaps the first industry to acknowledge the critical role of Purpose is the luxury industry. This is a sector that withstood economic booms and crisis, macro-shifts, industrial revolutions and even world wars. More recently, during the financial crisis and after the fall of Lehman Brothers in 2008, the luxury industry demonstrated its resilience once more, outperforming most other industries and even recovering much faster and stronger than any other industry.[105] According to a report by Bain & Company, the global personal luxury goods market held steady amid geopolitical uncertainty.[106] The luxury sector always understood that in order to build a market that is truly connected with the customer, company leaders needed to identify and articulate a shared Purpose that connected their organizations internally and externally. If we look at longstanding successful luxury brands, it becomes blatantly clear that Purpose is the secret ingredient in the elixir for uniqueness, independence, creating value far beyond the rationality of money and time.

How Luxury Brands Apply Purpose

"In the real world of work,
Purpose finding is what leaders do."

Prof. Robert E. Quinn

Professor Emeritus of Management and Organizations
University of Michigan's Ross School of Business

Against the backdrop of an ever more connected and empowered consumer, leaders, brands, products and messages serve as anchor points for entire belief systems. Therefore, demonstrating integrity in any form of business is no longer just an option, but mandatory to survival. Luxury brands are at the forefront of branding, fueling dreams and aspirations while simultaneously building loyalty and generating above average profit margins. Even during the financial crisis, luxury brands were growing at 10–15% annually.[107] How do they do it? What can we learn from this prosperous sector? In which ways do luxury business models differ from conventional ones?

As Rebecca Robins, Managing Director of Interbrand, wrote: "Over the past 15 years of the Best Global Brands list, the brand value amassed by luxury businesses has grown from $25.8 billion in 2000 to $143.7 billion in 2015. For well over a decade, luxury brands have ascended. They were hailed as haloed protectorates of double-digit growth. [...] When the economic crisis hit, luxury brands were the most resilient in weathering the storm."[108] We analyzed the common characteristics that helped luxury brands maintain stable growth and we discovered that they all have one thing in common: their unwavering anchorage to serve a higher Purpose rather than chasing short-term returns. Regardless of the economic climate, luxury brands have stayed loyal to who they really are; and more importantly, *why* they are. The luxury industry not only creates the finest objects and experiences, but its companies are also excellent at managing their core brand equity, or in other words, their internal 'Know-Why.' Luxury brands adopt a holistic mindset, always aware of the fact that Purpose must be integrated across all business functions. At first sight this might appear to be a conundrum, however, it is unquestionably the common denominator.

Not surprisingly, there is a growing tendency for non-luxury companies to recruit executives and directors from the luxury industry. Non-luxury organizations are interested in finding out how luxury brands build and maintain desirability and prosperity by harnessing the power emanating from a clearly defined and articulated Purpose. Tesla hired Burberry executive Ganesh Srivats as vice president of North American sales. Yves Saint Laurent's former CEO, Paul Deneve, went to Apple. Apple also hired Tag Heuer's Patrick Pruniaux and former Burberry CEO, Angela Ahrendts. A pattern is emerging to gather strategic intelligence from luxury brand experts.

One of the factors that help luxury brands stay on Purpose is upholding values. As many luxury brands are family businesses, long-term thinking is the normal mode of operandi. Not being subject to the same degree of external market forces, short-term pressure and stock market returns, a typical luxury business plan cycle spans five- to ten-years if not more. As Count Anton-Wolfgang von Faber-Castell said, "Well-run family companies are distinguished by sustainable values and human virtues." Quick fixes that satisfy immediate needs and ignore the scope of the future are not an accepted way of operating in the luxury industry.

In order to understand how Purpose is applied among luxury brands, we suggest looking at the strong relationship between the famous Blue Ocean Strategy[109] framework and the luxury business model: conventional competitive markets are the red oceans, turning market dynamics into one big bloodbath. Being preoccupied with competitors paralyzes the vision of a company, often even before it enters a particular market. Blue Ocean Strategy, to put it simply, is about aiming at either expanding the pie (the market) or finding a new pie altogether, rather than racing to get a slice of an existing one, thereby making competition irrelevant. This is where Blue Ocean Strategy and the luxury business model intersect. Both look beyond competition from the start. If there is something comparable on the market, it is no longer luxury since real luxury is, by definition, a superlative good or service. Luxury is about elevation. Louis XIV, French ruler in the 17th century and commonly known as Louis the Great or the Sun King, wore high heels to elevate himself. Whilst he was of very short stature, every nobleman of that time and regardless of height would have been wearing high heels. It was symbolic of their elevated status in society. Indeed, it is men who invented and wore high heels for many centuries before women adopted them, elevating their attractiveness and rightly so claiming equality in society. Elevation is about moving up in society, professionally, socially, economically and culturally.

Instead of aiming at creating a better product or service, luxury entrepreneurs are passionate about designing or inventing something that is at its pinnacle. Something that is not just better; but the best. Aiming for perfection, to create the best product possible and fill the universe around with desirability. Gradually, this universe becomes a kind of 'small monopoly' that is so desirable that it is beyond the realm of competition, creating an uncontested marketplace. Such a business model is based on being *bought from* rather than *selling to* – which liberates businesses and prevents them from falling into the unprofitable spiral of doing whatever the customer wants.

Luxury brands don't follow – they lead. Asking what consumers want is not part of Blue Ocean Strategy. This dynamic is not about giving customers what they want. As Henry Ford explained it nicely: "If I had asked people what they wanted, they would have said: faster horses." Instead, this is about creating something customers have not yet imagined.

131

For easy reference, we have grouped the dynamics of what distinguishes luxury propositions from conventional perspectives:

Antidotes of Luxury Marketing

Conventional Marketing	Luxury Marketing
Volume	Value
Loud signaling	Low signaling
Foreground	Background
Content marketing	Brand journalism
Quantity	Quality
Overpromising	Understatement
Demographic segment	Psychographic segment
Mass marketing	Niche marketing
Popular influencers	Key influencers
Fast communication	Slow communication
Short-term mindset	Long-term mindset
Buying audience	Building audience
Mathematical progress	Geometrical progress
Expansionist growth	Vertical growth
Red Ocean Strategy	Blue Ocean Strategy
Comparative decisions	Superlative decisions

Continuous learning, transforming and refining Know-How is an important factor that determines the timelessness of a brand. Luxury brands are brilliant at this. In their article on the scholastic nature of luxury, Andrew Shipilov and Frédéric Godart look at conglomerates LVMH, Kering and Richemont. They explain how participants of training programs usually don't realize that they are in a program at all. The best part about such training programs is that there is no single authority that teaches. The protégé, the disciple, the trainee or the apprentice is the scholar, but also the wise one with valuable knowledge. The only teacher or mentor is the learner's inner dynamo that works through self-observation, introspection, self-examination, critical thinking, self-analysis and intrinsic integrity. The learner is forced to take the truth as the authority instead of taking the authority as the truth.

Many fashion brands manufacture their products in Third World countries, primarily to save costs. Because they often chase volume over quality and integrity in what they offer, they run the risk of becoming a victim of controversy and scandal. Fashion products have short lifecycles, are subject to market trends and as a consequence, products come and go as quickly as the season changes. Adopting the principles of timelessness could shift fashion brands into a Purpose-driven transformation process. Hard to do, but possible at the cost of reverse-engineering existing paradigms and structures, requiring a bold move to abandon short-term pressures.

Luxury brands are hardly dependent on technology, yet they still operate very successfully. Even having the latest technology in your organization will not help you withstand economic turbulence, nor will it transform your brand into something meaningful and timeless, especially if your brand still lacks an overarching Purpose. Customer Relationship Management (CRM) is becoming CMR (Customer Managed Relationships), meaning the customer decides when, what and how to communicate or buy. CRM today is about adopting the right mindset and building an internal culture first, rather than just installing the right software.

Startups and Tech companies can learn from luxury in other areas too. Take Tesla for instance, and its meticulous attention to both design and distribution. Luxury brands operate vertically integrated value chains. In the same spirit that Hermés owns its stores, Elon Musk is cleverly building an integrated value chain, which costs a fortune (Tesla does not operate a 'franchise' system and 'owns' its distribution), but it gives them the competitive advantage of being able to manage the entire customer experience very tightly. Other technology brands operate outside the conventional thinking methods of their sector too, including Apple and Nest (which was acquired by Google). What they all have in common is a strong sense of aesthetics, which they have applied to both product design and their business model. They have learnt from luxury brands how to align Purpose throughout the entire organization.

Fast Moving Consumer Goods (FMCG) can benefit from taking a closer look at luxury, too. FMCG marketing works in the complete opposite direction to the world of luxury. For example, Veuve Clicquot revolutionized biodegradable, isothermal packaging as a demonstration of integrity and quality in their production processes. While the number of people consuming Veuve Clicquot champagne is dramatically smaller than the number of people buying smartphones, for instance, there are still many FMCG companies that are not environmentally and sustainably active. As the name implies, FMCG is generally a game of speed, volume, oversupply, discounts and thin margins, resulting in millions of waste in a world that is in desperate need for environmental and ecological awareness as well as sustainable community development.

Advertisements from finance companies often lack creativity and aesthetics in their messages. This is generally due to the fact that most finance companies make large investments in marketing but very little in branding. Pure rationality leaves no room for subjectivity and creative exploration. Working integrity inside out is key in an environment where consumer trust is at an all-time low. A change of value and belief systems and tapping into the transformational power of a brand could do wonders for the finance industry as a whole. Environments such as banking, asset management, private equity, hedge funds, etc. are driven by numbers, generally excluding qualitative analysis, subjective interpretation and behavioral economics. Consequently, the ability to create desire by connecting on a deeper, emotional level is often non-existent. In a time where AI is on the fast track and algorithms have the potential to replace core-banking propositions, it would be wise for financial institutions to rethink their positioning and underpinning value systems. We shall explore the intricacies of this notion in depth further on.

For now, let's hold the thought that contemporary brand management does one thing really well: putting the customer at the heart of thinking.

21st Century Customer Centricity

*"Get closer than ever to your customers.
So close that you tell them what they need
well before they realize it themselves."*

Steve Jobs
Founder of Apple

Between the years 1850 and 1950, the world navigated through the age of industrialization. These times were based on a 'take to market' business model. Finding customers in an era where demand never ceased was not hard. Companies were primarily engineering-led and product-oriented, and the notion of truly understanding the customer was practically non-existent.

At some point in the late 1930s, Procter & Gamble recognized the need to differentiate and actively 'brand manage' products in order to optimize market orientation and financial returns, articulating the first notion of modern brand management. As competition started to pick up, the idea of 'positioning' emerged. Targeting and ideally occupying a specific place in the minds of consumers required an innate understanding of how consumers tick. Whilst somewhat more consumer-centric, this is still essentially a one-way approach to capturing markets (and customers). We call this the 'market to' era, taking us to about the year 2000.

Since then, businesses have started to recognize that putting the customer at the heart of their value propositions is the way to thrive in the future. This marks the beginning of the post- positioning era, moving past the 'take to market' and 'market to' approaches. Essentially, brands must step beyond the idea of understanding consumers (think about market research, focus groups, etc.) and embrace the concept of co-creating value with consumers. Developing a product, testing it, and then taking it to market no longer suffices. Value creation starts in unison with the customer.

From Product Centricity to Co-creation of Value with Customers

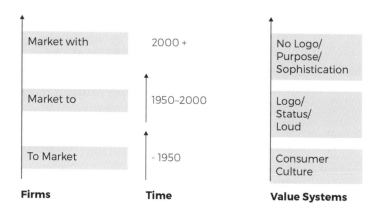

Case in Point: Harley-Davidson

Founded over a century ago in a shed in Milwaukee just north of Chicago, Harley-Davidson has emerged as a brand with the ability to withstand the test of time. Its power lies in the strength of its Purpose, one that has inspired generations past and present by offering a world of socially accepted rebellion based on values of freedom and independence. Like many companies of the era, Harley-Davidson was created by engineers who were passionate about the burgeoning possibilities technology offered.

Their first motorcycle was called the Silent Gray Fellow, a very reliable 'bicycle with an engine' that got you from A to B. Taking the Silent Gray

Fellow 'to market' won the company a positive reputation: customer demand for the company's products picked up, especially during and after World War I when military demand for motorcycles further propelled the company's growth.

It wasn't until the late 1930s that Harley-Davidson realized the fundamental shift that would eventually change its course of business. Simply taking products to market was no longer good enough in a market where most Americans bought automobiles instead, or at least aspired to own one. Understanding what customers wanted early on, the company boldly repositioned its brand image as a lifestyle choice, rather than a means of transportation. The marketing approach shifted towards a purposeful 'to customers' focus, moving away from a rational 'to market' one. Movies like *Easy Rider* or even *Terminator* underpinned the rebellious nature of what the brand stood for and customers soon no longer bought Harley-Davidson for the function of the product itself, but instead for the experience the brand provided. Harley-Davidson managed to revise their story to one that allowed customers to break out of their daily routines and enjoy the freedom of the open road with like-minded peers – a message that resonated with the changing needs of customers.

In 2013, Harley-Davidson launched 'Project Rushmore,' a large-scale initiative embedding a customer value creation framework into their product development process by involving hundreds of riders from all over the world. Customer feedback was taken into the heart of the development process for the company's next generation of motorcycles. It's certainly not an easy feat for a century-old brand to stay relevant in the 21st century – and it doesn't happen by chance. It requires focus, dedication and the courage to see beyond the obvious to be able to successfully take a brand from the era of 'Build it and they will come'[110] to a place where 'Built by All of us, for All of us'[111] creates major appeal for customers.

In today's globally connected and complex economy, true differentiation on a product or service level is getting ever harder to achieve – not everyone is Apple. Even Tesla is starting to struggle as the incumbent automotive players are catching up to produce similar, if not better, electric cars. For most businesses and brand leaders, the recognition is one of consternation: most products and services today are identical or marginally differentiated at best. The age of creating truly Unique Selling Propositions (USP) is long gone. But while true differentiation is ever harder to achieve, the opportunity of creating Unique Value Propositions (UVP) is much more realistic. Adjusting your focus on UVP vs USP might appear subtle, but it's a powerful perspective to adopt.

Taking a customer centric approach to communicating value propositions is important, but not intuitive. Firstly, it helps to recall how basic brand and marketing communication works. Perhaps the simplest way to conceptualize this is the AIDA model. It essentially states that each customer journey starts with a (future) customer becoming aware of a product or service, followed by an expressed interest that translates (hopefully) into desire, leading to purchase (action).

The AIDA Framework

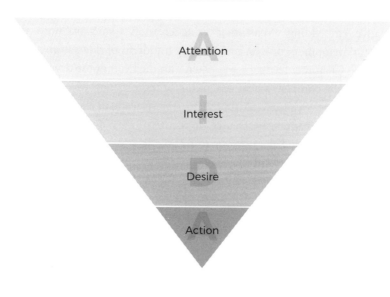

The idea is to structure communication in a relevant way at each stage of the AIDA journey, ultimately leading to loyal customers who repeat purchase. It is an effective framework to help validate almost any communications concept.

This simple approach is expanded with the *The Customer Centricity Framework.*[112] Rather than a funnel working from top-down as in the AIDA model above, it serves as a guiding tool that assumes a linear customer journey, from left to right. From awareness (Seed) to interest (Prospect) to Conversion (Customer) to Loyalty (Repeat Purchase).

The Customer Centricity Framework

We can now connect the customer journey with two distinct spheres: the awareness and the experience spaces. These spheres intersect and overlap at the point of conversion. Communications activities can be distinctively orchestrated to be relevant at any given touchpoint.

For example: broad targeting activities that aim at increasing brand or product awareness, such as TV or Display Ads on Google, will be used to get attention and create interest at the seed and prospecting stage. Special events or actual product experiences such as test-drives for cars for instance are marketing tactics that will be used to increase desire and move a prospect from being interested in purchasing to become a customer. Regular communication activities such as newsletters or magazines for example serve to retain customers in our universe and help strengthen the bond for increased loyalty and retention.

It can't be overemphasized how important it is to understand the underlying concept of how to make communication relevant for a given audience. Whilst simple and tactical, both the AIDA model and the Customer Centricity Framework can serve well when thinking through how to communicate effectively. Especially when complexity increases, simple thinking-structures like these can be of tremendous help to better cope with the rapidly changing nature of the marketing discipline.

The Changing Nature of Consumers

*"Some people think luxury is the opposite of poverty.
It is not. It is the opposite of vulgarity."*

Coco Chanel
French Fashion Designer and Businesswoman

When exploring what drives change, it is often helpful to adopt an outside perspective. Looking at broader shifts on how customers, brands and their propositions evolve is what provides the strategic canvas. Whilst the luxury industry is looking at how the consumer landscape changes for them, we believe it is actually worthwhile looking at this very sector and the luxury customer of today in order to understand how consumers will behave in the future.

Luxury propositions are successful because they sit outside the rationale of value for money. They promise to belong to an aspirational world, loaded with emotion, richness, depth and stability. Such brands can help us see beyond conventional wisdom, altering the way we think about marketing today. Full of heritage, history and legacy, luxury brands do not radically change. However, they do evolve and modernize to keep up with the times.

In the height of today's information overload, access to knowledge about luxury has never been broader. It comes as no surprise that many luxury brands have been quick to jump on the digital bandwagon, offering anything from Skype interviews with craftsmen to virtual 360° tours of their ateliers. Whilst digitalization is becoming more important for luxury brands, the growing attitude among luxury consumers is that offline is today's new luxury.

For generations born before the 1950s, Tesla or Apple may not fully fit the definition of true luxury. However, the complex but romantic relationship between luxury and technology is gradually strengthening for the post-Baby Boomer generations. Rolls Royce, for instance, organized a free exhibition in Saatchi & Saatchi London where visitors could interact with and experience the technological expression of their Spirit of Ecstasy.[113]

Among Millennials and the upcoming Generation Z, experientialism is already the new existentialism. In other words, status is changing. Status is a transitional concept: what was once seen as a demonstration of power (think of Louis XIV and his status demonstration of social power, elevating himself by means of wearing high heels) has morphed into proof of status through the demonstration of wealth (as in 'let me show you my shiny, super-fast red car'), to status being a demonstration of taste and sophistication.

In a sense then, being in the know is the new way of showing status. Let's explore the implications of this in more depth:

From Existentialism To Experientialism[114]

From	To
buy	live
sharing economy	opinion economy
status	taste
communication	connection
own	experience
online moments	offline moments
show	know

In the US – which is the largest luxury market in the world – we can observe for the first time in history that affluent Americans of Generation X outnumber Baby Boomers, according to Ipsos' Affluent Survey.[115] So yes, it is fair to claim that as the luxury consumer changes, so does the concept of luxury – but it is not because of technology, digitalization or social media. Luxury goods are still mainly purchased offline. The underlying driver is a craving for value – not as in 'value for money,' but as in 'value of meaning.' The evidence pointing to this can be found in geographies with a younger consumer demographic: 71% of consumers in India and 80% of consumers in China are prepared to pay a premium price for products with a Purpose.[116]

This dynamic becomes most evident when observing how new brands are being tested and tried by Millennials – and increasingly by the post-Millennial consumers, too. When they try a new luxury brand, product, hotel or a fine-dining restaurant, one of the first things Generation Y and Z will look for is LEGS – Lifestyle Enrichment Goods and Services. For luxury (brands) it means going beyond function, beyond the aspirational brand worlds and beyond promises of status. In a nutshell, LEGS represents the customer's search for meaning. And it is being put to the test 24/7 and without mercy.

According to the Airbus Billionaire Study[117], those new to wealth are generally more impulsive, but over time they become more discerning. The desire for silent luxury has existed for years in European economies and we've started witnessing similar patterns in the Asian markets about five years ago. A well-known logo and a high price tag are no longer enough – discernment, sophistication and taste are the new norm. Indeed, this is the transition from Show to Know.

Customers are increasingly choosing brands based on inner meaning and holistic integrity, rather than look and feel or symbolic value. This trend is particularly apparent in China. A growing middle class, striving for equality and access to information is yielding a progressively sophisticated customer base. Russia and Middle Eastern markets are also traveling down this road, albeit at a slower pace.

***The Evolution of Taste and the Implications on the
Changing Nature of Luxury Clientele***

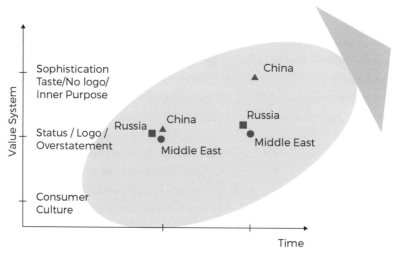

Time will tell how the next generation of luxury consumers in emerging economies will translate the idea of sophistication and taste. New research by Dr Stephen Kraus,[118] SVP of Ipsos, also validates that today 'subtle and understated' are among the building blocks of affluent luxury customers' interest.

As luxury continues to be democratized, more consumers will look to enter the markets for sophistication and taste rather than the pure rationality of monetary value. Brands, companies and individuals with clarity of Purpose are changing the world for the better.

Intelligent Impact Investors (3Is)

"Always look for durable competitive advantage."

Charlie Munger
American investor,
VC of Berkshire Hathaway

A son of an entrepreneur behind a successful restaurant chain asked his father the following question: "Why don't you invest in the oil business, the stocks, shipping or the global arms trade? Aren't they the best industries with the largest returns?" His father then replied to his son saying: "The best industry to invest in, my son, is the one in which only you can excel."

According to the British economist John Kay, most objectives are best pursued tangentially or indirectly. For instance, founders of luxury brands never really focused on ways of making profits. They invested on ways and means of creating the best object and the corresponding experience to go with it. Growing profits were a byproduct of that investment, rather than the objective. Were they to be preoccupied with trying harder to make more profits, they would likely weaken their position. On a more operational level, when it comes to investing effort and time, the Italian economist Vilfredo Pareto had a point when formulating the 80-20 rule. He noted that 80% of the reward comes from 20% of the effort. Identifying and prioritizing that valuable 20% makes all the difference in investing. Serving as a North Star, the Guiding Purpose Strategy guides one in deciding where to concentrate resources or, in other words, in identifying that very valuable 20%.

As briefly outlined in previous chapters, Purpose and profit are not opposites. Leveraging the guidance stemming from a clearly defined core Purpose also allows to direct energy and effort more effectively. It makes the space needed to create authentic distinction, long-term attitude, singularity and originality and other, so called, monopolistic traits that can transcend competition, economic crisis and other external factors. An area where this becomes very apparent is Impact investing. Impact investment is essentially about unleashing the power of capital to do good in addition to generating monetary returns.[119] Such businesses, as intelligent impact investors (3Is) agree, are worthy of investing. Such businesses are, in many ways, irreplaceable, incomparable and inimitable (3Is).

For example, the intelligent investor Warren Buffet, CEO of Berkshire Hathaway, has always been interested in buying companies that have monopolistic traits: high pricing power, substantial competitive advantage and a strong brand identity[120]. Or as R. Hargreaves observed: "Looking back at his most transformative investments of all time, it is clear that at the time he invested, these companies were not market leaders, but they did have the edge over peers." Many other intelligent investors as i.e. Charles Munger or Benjamin Graham would most likely concur.

One of the most powerful means to attract investment is the ability to create a positive reputation. Investors give far more importance to reputational factors than financial considerations when responding to corporate crises, according to research from FTI Consulting. The report suggests that, "emotional drivers heavily outweigh financial ones." 100 corporate crises were studied to see how investors react. One hundred and thirty investors were asked about their main drivers for responding to a profit warning: only 28% pointed to financial reasons[121]. Investors like other stakeholders are behavioral beings and don't act purely rational.

Last but not least, long-term visions make minds think alike. The strategic long-termism of timeless brands makes way for thinking ahead of the times, which clarifies their future. Since this approach then reduces the gamble about what's ahead it boosts the confidence of investors' decision-making too. Competitive advantage alone isn't sufficient. It is durable competitive advantage that makes all the difference in the world.

Purpose for the Financial Industry

"The end of one era is the beginning of a new one."

Jean-Francois Hirschel
Contributing Author, Founder of H-Ideas

Since the Global Financial Crisis of 2008, the financial sector has undergone a profound transformation and its reputation is at stake. Is it the end of capitalism in the traditional sense of the word? For sure, financial institutions have a higher Purpose than to just make money for their shareholders. Have they done the necessary work to clearly identify and express their Purpose? Is this enough to re-establish the trust they need to attract new clients, to keep the ones they have and to build the committed teams they need to tackle the challenges of a world in transformation? In this chapter we will review the specific role of Purpose in the financial industry and assess how it can help address some of the challenges of the sector. The particular case of asset managers will be reviewed, based on an in-depth analysis of how they project what they do in terms of Responsible Investment in their brand: the Hirschel & Kramer Responsible Investment Brand Index, or RIBI™ for short.

The financial industry faces numerous challenges. Since Lehman's collapse more than ten years ago, Central Banks have fueled the world with 'free liquidity' to sustain growth, thereby triggering an environment of low interest rates. An environment which is structurally here to stay because of the ageing demographics of developed economies. With such rates, the room for maneuvering in order to create margins is thin.

Advances in technology are also shaking up the financial world: will internet-based robots replace the traditional bank branches which are part of the urban landscape? Will blockchain technology render a whole set of intermediaries involved in a transaction settlement redundant? Will the next celebrity of finance be an artificial intelligence algorithm, rather than Warren Buffet?

Above all, the main challenge the financial industry needs to address is its reputation – the need to build trust with existing customers, to establish long-term mutually profitable relationships with them and also to attract new clients. This then creates its own challenge, namely, to build a team of highly skilled, motivated and committed employees. Tellingly, as the latest "LinkedIn's 10 Most Desirable Global Companies to Work For" ranking shows, no financial institutions are part of this top league.

LinkedIn's 10 Most Desirable Global Companies to Work For.[122]

1. Amazon
2. Alphabet
3. Facebook
4. Salesforce
5. Tesla
6. Apple
7. Comcast NBC Universal
8. The Walt Disney Company
9. Oracle
10. Netflix

Undoubtedly there has been a profound shift from 1970 when Milton Friedman, winner of the Nobel Prize for Economics, wrote an article in the *New York Times* entitled 'The Social Responsibility of Business is to Increase its Profits'[123] to what Larry Fink, CEO of Blackrock, the largest asset manager in the world wrote in his annual letter to CEOs in 2018: "Society is increasingly turning to the private sector and asking that companies respond to broader societal challenges."[124] Practice what you preach. What Larry Fink asks of the CEOs of the companies asset managers invest in, should hold true, first and foremost, for the asset managers themselves.

We can't think of any industry other than asset management that is better placed to "respond to broader societal challenges." On the one hand, given they manage our assets, investment managers are a major player in the financial well-being of our ageing population. On the other hand, through the investments they make, they have an impact on society and can actively manage this impact.

There is also a regulatory aspect to this subject. The UK Corporate Governance Code for example, published by the Financial Reporting Council in July 2018, states that "The board should establish the company's Purpose, values and strategy, and satisfy itself that these and its culture are aligned."

Consequently, we wanted to take a look at how asset managers project their inner Purpose in their brand. For sure, the Purpose of an asset manager goes beyond "Generating good financial performance." It comes perhaps as no surprise that few asset managers express a Purpose, even less a Purpose which connects with societal goals.

Responsible Investment is one-way asset managers can respond to broader societal challenges. It covers numerous goals, practices and ways to manage money, one of the most well-known being ESG investment, ESG standing for "Environment, Social, Governance." Today this approach attracts increasing interest from investors, with global assets under management in ESG having grown by a third in the two years from 2016 to 2018.[125]

We analyzed the largest European Asset Managers and evaluated them using two metrics: what they commit to in terms of Responsible Investment, and how they project this in their brand. This is the H&K Responsible Investment Brand Index, whose detailed methodology and results can be found on www.ri-brandindex.org.

The overall results of the 2019 edition can be summarized as follows:

Responsible Investment Brand Index RIBI™ 2019

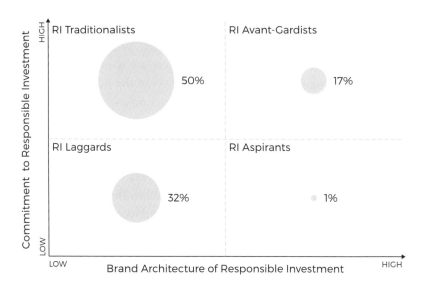

The Avant-Gardists who come out above average, both in terms of commitment to Responsible Investment and in terms of Brand Architecture of Responsible Investment, represent 17% of this largest European Asset Managers sample. We looked at them from a size standpoint and found that size is actually not a factor: you don't need to be big to be a Responsible Investment Avant-Gardist. Conversely, being small and nimble is not an advantage either. From a geography standpoint, we found that French and Swiss companies are slightly more present in the Avant-Gardist category than their natural market weight. Conversely, German companies are underrepresented.

The bulk of the companies (50%) fall into the Traditionalists category, meaning they have committed to Responsible Investment but do not yet project this commitment in their brand.

We have looked more precisely at Purpose and found out that 40% of the asset managers in our sample express a Purpose. Referring back to Larry

Fink's statement that "society is demanding that companies, both public and private, serve a social Purpose", we found only 13% of asset managers articulate a Purpose which has a connection with society.

Are these disappointing results? One can always hope for better, for sure. Let's not forget, this is a relatively recent trend, and let's not forget that the financial industry is still not very familiar with the concepts of brand, identity and Purpose. By its very nature, the financial sector relies on facts and figures to make decisions and is less used to dealing with emotions and feelings. Nevertheless, clients make their buying decisions based on sentiment and feelings.

By way of example, here are a few Purpose statements that did score highly in the RIBI™ Index.

- "Our goal is to help people invest better, retire better." (Hermes Investment Management)

- "To empower people to live a better life." (AXA Investment Managers)

- "We believe investing responsibly enables economic prosperity and social progress." (State Street Global Advisors)

"No emotion. No decision."[126] As years of research in neurobiology show, our buying decisions are based on emotion. They are explained, justified and rationalized by facts and figures, but emotion triggers the buy button. Speaking only of the asset management industry and Europe, there are some 4,000 managers pursuing the same clients. And there are 54,000 funds that these clients can choose from.[127] Standing out from the crowd is paramount, and this isn't simply a case of loudly stating "My performance is better than my neighbor's." These claims don't last... A genuine Purpose expressed clearly and ambitiously, reveals the true identity of an entity, and differentiates it accordingly. Companies, like humans, are unique. They are their history; they are their culture. To be differentiating is about being able to identify these aspects and expressing them succinctly inside and outside.

Would you agree that the Purpose statement cited above, "To empower people to live a better life" looks at things from a higher perspective than "We will deliver good returns" (all the more so as this latter statement will doubtless be accompanied by a lengthy legal disclaimer)?

Can we imagine a world where a reporting document about the management of an individual's wealth will be made of several pages of impact statements (such as CO_2 reduction, compensation fairness, equality in education) – and the financial performance statement will be just an appendix? This is ambitious, and maybe even utopian, but several major driving forces are heading in this direction. This is also a way for asset managers to connect with their clients, speaking passionately about topics they care about and using language they understand, rather than financial jargon.

We have acknowledged that the reputation of the financial industry is at stake. Setting objectives beyond the power of the balance sheet and positioning itself as a major driver of a harmonious society is an opportunity for this industry to become the enabler of what goes right, rather than the scapegoat of everything which goes wrong. Identifying a Purpose connected with societal objectives and living up to it is the foundation of such a mindset. It is a huge responsibility for the sector to embrace this societal and industry trend in the most ethical way possible.

Attaining and Retaining Reputation

"Money is the McMansion in Sarasota that looks good
and starts falling apart after a few years.
Power is the old stone building
that stands for centuries."

Francis Underwood
protagonist of *House of Cards*

As a science of strategy, game theory is so efficient that historically speaking, clever figures with analytical abilities as such as Dr John Dee, advisor to the Queen, would get arrested for crimes of 'calculating.'[128] For the same reason even today in some societies where religious dogma is still present, the intellectual game of chess is declared as forbidden.

The commonality here is that value systems drive culture. Open, evolving ecosystems appear to be better able at adapting to changing context and hence can weave the path to future prosperity. Restriction will generally hinder progress. The theory we put forward is that reputation is earned and hence comes from within. It is not about projection, but about continuously demonstrating integrity in everything one does. When seen against this dynamic then, inner value systems that drive 'right' behavior is fundamental to attaining and maintaining a positive reputation.

Identifying the key categories of organizations that have both deep reputability and have achieved significant longevity, we can look at the common denominators amongst them. It is apparent that there are shared characteristics among the approaches of traditional institutions such as the Vatican Church or the United Grand Lodge of England, as well as academic institutions such as the long-established universities and heritage-oriented luxury brands such as Breguet or Hennesy for instance.

Their sine qua non components for economic longevity are:

- Long-term commitment

- Evolutionary stability

- Mentor-mentee tradition

- Being guided by timeless verities

- Taking slow but sure steps

- Internal culture led by universal values

Long-term commitment, evolutionary stability, the mentor-mentee tradition, being guided by timeless verities, taking slow but sure steps and internal cultures led by universal values lead to durable trusted reputation.

Family values and inter-generational thinking is also a classic characteristic of deeply reputable companies that enjoy economic longevity. They tend to comprehend the intricacies of long termism better than others. Thus, they can see what's far ahead of them. For instance, the ex-CEO of Faber-Castell, a 260-year-old brand, Count Anton-Wolfgang von Faber-Castell, explained this by saying: "We family entrepreneurs naturally find it easier to think in terms of generations and to see through projects whose fruits will not be reaped for perhaps decades, and only after setbacks. In a listed company, this attitude would have got me fired at least three times by now, especially in the days when shareholder value was the be-all and end-all, and the goal of short-term profit eclipsed any long-term considerations."[129]

History has shown that brands with deep reputability and strong value-systems pass the test of time, not only in the sense that they don't die but also in the sense that they tend to stand above the economic ups and downs. It is important to acknowledge that these common characteristics function only when they are lived deeply. In other words, merely talking about them or putting them in a lofty sounding mission/vision section on a website will not go far. But the impact of experience and evidence on reputation does last: I believe it when I see it. Manners maketh the brand.

Vital Integrity in Communications

"Moving from words to action is the ultimate proof of integrity."

Reto Zangerl
Contributing Author,
Founder of Brand Affairs

When asked what he looks for in new recruits, business magnate and investor Warren Buffet replied "energy, intelligence and integrity," adding that "if you don't have the latter, the first two will kill you." But integrity is not only essential in investing and recruitment – it is fundamental to communications, too.

Why? We are living in a hyper-communicative age when the influence of major institutions such as the state, church, schools and family is in decline. Markets are overcrowded and there is a distracting abundance of choice. In theory, more information would create less uncertainty. But as we can see in the current global economy with its clamor of voices, fake news and information overload, complexity only increases. Many people know a little about multiple topics but only a few develop in-depth knowledge.

Investors, entrepreneurs and strategists keep their finger on the pulse of an industry before making an important business move – gathering the necessary knowledge, if not intelligence, to fulfill their goals. However, in an environment where it is ever harder to distinguish genuine information from subjective or indeed outright wrong information, there is a pressing need for objectivity and clarity. Consequently, there is a stronger need for firmness, certainty and reliability.

Brands can jump into this gap and help employees and customers discover direction, values and orientation. Strong brands grow and create value for employees and consumers by creating an identity, revealing huge opportunities that go well beyond their actual service or product to engage with stakeholders on a more meaningful level. It is their fundamental *integrity* that forms their behavior in everything they do. No wonder they tend to outperform their competitors.

But what is integrity in this context? The Cambridge Dictionary defines integrity as: '*the quality of being honest and having strong moral principles that you refuse to change.*'

Companies with integrity have a strong moral compass guiding all their decisions and actions. They are well aware that sometimes it takes unpopular decisions to earn trust, and sometimes it is necessary to make decisions that only bear fruit in the long run. Integrity demands truthfulness and honesty. It inspires people to rely on you, as they know you will keep your promises. In some cases, it means telling the truth even if the truth is difficult. Integrity means showing a consistent, non-negotiable and uncompromising adherence to strong moral principles and ethical values.

The ancient Egyptians had labyrinth rituals. The selected would go into the labyrinth with the aim of not getting lost. They used a simple secret formula: if you start going to the right you have to keep going right all the time. In this way, even if you make mistakes, you at least know that you made a mistake by going right. But if you make a right, then a left, and then a right turn, things become complicated and you quickly become lost. In many ways, this is a navigational lesson about firmness and consistency, which are among the components that form the foundation of integrity.

In an age of omni-connection, more data and, consequently, more transparency, there is a growing need for brands with integrity. What can brands do to deal with this reality?

First and foremost, integrity is closely tied to leadership.[130] Absolute integrity and ensuing trust can only develop in a company where the management team and owners fully align, acting as beacons and role models for the organization to develop. Secondly, brands and companies need to make sure they attract and retain the right people. Since brands and companies radiate from within, integrity is perhaps the most important factor when hiring a new team member. However, integrity is typically also an innate quality and it cannot be the role of organizations to 'teach integrity.' Brands and companies do have the responsibility however to provide cohesive and comprehensive behavioral boundaries that act as a strong, collective moral compass.

An internal moral compass is an invaluable resource that makes clear to everyone what integrity means for the company and how the organization can progress with it. But most of all, promises must be kept. Moving from words to action and delivering on every detail of your commitments is the ultimate proof of integrity.

Growth: Spiraling Upwards

"The empires of the future are the empires of the mind."

Sir Winston Churchill
British statesman &
Nobel Prize Laureate for Literature

Expanding production quantity, expanding the team, the number of offices or stores around the world, extending to all kinds of categories of products and services... all of these are characteristics of expansionist growth. However, what is frequently forgotten is that real growth has a vertical nature. A tree grows upwards. A child grows taller. An individual human being is a vertical species that stands tall, looking like the letter 'I.' A student that decides to be in the scholarly vertical path can become a teacher, then get a Master's degree, then a PhD and finally become a Professor. Social or professional self-realization entails vertical ascension.

Horizontal growth is an almost endless expansion as opposed to elevation. Employing a larger number of people does not necessarily mean increased productivity or improved performance, but it definitely means increased complexity. In order to raise the quality of the internal culture in an organization and make relations more harmonious it is key to minimize complexity. Studies focusing on how structures, networks and interaction patterns can promote cooperation in biology and in society can be applied to business, too: a few strong ties are better than a million weak ones.[131]

The British anthropologist Robin Dunbar introduced the rule of 150, which is a cognitive limit to the number of people with whom one can maintain stable social relationships. Numbers larger than this generally require more restrictive rules, laws, and enforced norms to maintain a stable, cohesive group. Naturally, this number has implications in the context of organizational growth, too: it is not about the quantity but about the quality of relations. In simple terms, when an organization or a network grows to more than 150, it runs the risks of dilution, silo thinking, alienation of why you are here, leading to different agendas, lack of coherence and so forth. The weakness of relationships increases. Going beyond 150 is not directly proportional. Or in other words, these effects do not amplify much further whether looking at growth in groups from to 200 or 5,000.

Organizations that are interested in vertical growth are those that get rid of the hamster wheels and apply a golden-section approach growth. So instead of going around the same circles and cycles, they are spiraling upwards making paradigm shifts, advancing, increasing the quality (and often the price) of their services and the quality of life within their organizations. One of the main advantages of vertical growth is that, unlike in expansionist growth, there is less preoccupation with competition. Unlike horizontal growth, vertical growth is about Solomonian constructivism rather than faster and bloodier competition. Vertical growth is preoccupied with flight. Horizontal with fight.

So, what do organizations that aim at vertical growth do better?

It is, first of all, important to acknowledge that scale or size doesn't necessarily make an organization the market leader. In Bain&Co's analysis across 45 markets worldwide, the best companies – the economic leaders in their industries – are not always the biggest. Today, 40% of economic leaders are not scale leaders.[132]

As an illustration, a well-known example of vertical growth is the city of Florence. It didn't have an empire, but it had an empyreal approach. It is a very small city. Nevertheless, when one measures the disproportionately large impact it had on the rest of the world one begins to see how vertical growth works its magic. The Americas were named after a Florentine explorer and financier Amerigo Vespucci. (The USA too was discovered by a Florentine named Giovanni da Verrazzano.) Florence is the cradle of the European Renaissance. It introduced academic traditions that are alive to this day. It taught the world numerous arts and sciences. It built powerful bridges between investment, commerce and culture. No wonder its cultural influence in the world is present still today. Brands and organizations can learn a lot from the Florentine approach.

In order to better grasp the vertical growth approach to leadership, it is perhaps best to zoom in to the specific business model of boutique brands. Boutique businesses focus on organized, vertical growth. A good example is Roja Parfums, founded by the renowned perfumer and fragrance historian Roja Dove. Another good example is Officina Profumo Farmaceutica Santa Maria Novella. These brands may not be among the biggest players in the perfume industry, yet they are accepted to be among the finest in the perfume world.

A boutique-minded approach allows for greater focus. The report for the 2017–2021 on global luxury apparel confirms that pure-play luxury retailers are the leaders in the global personal luxury goods market.[133] In luxury brand management, instead of the business pushing a brand's growth, the brand yields growth for the business.

Boutique organizations tend to have less bureaucracy, decision-making is faster, more commitment and thought is put forward in finding solutions, attention to detail is higher, and the consciousness in spending capital is more selective. At the boutique level, margins for error are smaller – companies have to get it right the first time. This is one of the many reasons why the BMWs and VWs of today's global economy acquire organizations that have been able to keep their boutique spirit and founder's mentality alive. It is like buying a division or a department for the organization. However, it is not that easy: typically, 70%–90% of acquisitions fail.[134] What appears to be an accelerator bringing new skills in house or boost the company's competitive position falls short of expectations. What makes sense on spreadsheets falls a part in real life. It's a consequence of prioritizing the economic level over the cultural level. The key lies in the ability of retaining that boutique spirit.

Organized vertical growth or spiraling upwards is a key component of the elevationist approach. For companies recognizing this the future is not ahead, it is above.

GPS
Guiding Purpose Strategy

Decoding and Assembling Purpose

"The two most important days in our life
are the day you are born and the day you find out why."

Mark Twain
American Writer, Entrepreneur and Lecturer

In relation to businesses, value and meaning were once simple concepts contained in the practical aspects of a product or a service. A formula was followed whereas the functionality and utility offered would define the value, where the product was the brand and where the teams and people who delivered it were deeply connected with this modest but effective framework.

We live in times of tremendous change, macro-disruption and hyper-connectivity. As a consequence, we face a host of challenges and distractions that can result in misalignment, fragmentation, silo mentality, and in extreme cases, high-stress and dysfunctional environments.

As the boundaries of our personal and professional lives merge ever more closely together, it is imperative that we look for inspiring and collectively aligned meaning in what we do. But what is meaningful – what does, and should it mean? How do we define and measure it – and most importantly, how can we find, articulate and embed Purpose within our organizations, brands or indeed within ourselves?

According to the Big Innovation Centre, Britain's businesses could unlock up to US$170b (GBP£130b) were they to set and pursue a clear corporate Purpose.[135] We are certain that this figure is just as relevant to many other economies as well. Differentiation, brand essence, positioning and raison d'être are often conflated. Actually, they complement each other and should be seen as extensions. It is the innermost Purpose however, that symbolically represents the divine force within a business.

We are living in an age wherein Know-How must be complemented with Know-Where and most of all, with Know-Why. The Know-Why of Purpose serves as the North Star, a guiding force that is constant and reliable in an ever-changing world. Purpose lies at the essence of a brand and is a pre-condition to shape brand vision, business architecture and ultimately a new kind of competitive edge crucial to a conscious 21st century business management: culture.

Over time, lasting differentiation hinges on a company's ability to continuously innovate and perform. This is not about a unique product or service, but about building strength through a company's unique configuration of people – or in other words, its culture. Whilst distributed IP and globally connected markets allow for ever more rapid replication and scale of products and services, a company's culture cannot be copied easily. Or in the words of Prof. Peter Drucker: "Culture eats Strategy for Breakfast."

The following chapters will outline the process of creating a cohesive, well thought through *Guiding Purpose Strategy*.

The GPS Framework

"Experience is the teacher of all things."

Julius Caesar
Roman Politician and General

The Guiding Purpose Strategy Framework is the result of many years of first-hand experience of testing and adjusting methods and processes to help leading companies find clarity and alignment from within. The *GPS Framework* is structured as a three-layered rose. The central part of the rose is deep brand Purpose. The middle layer is composed of values, and the outer layer consists of language business leaders understand more commonly: vision, strategy, goals, etc. All elements interact in a continuum of forward motion, left to right.

Most people are comfortable with expressing tangible methods of 'how they do' things. It is therefore easiest to begin from the outer layer and work inwards.

The Guiding Purpose Strategy Framework

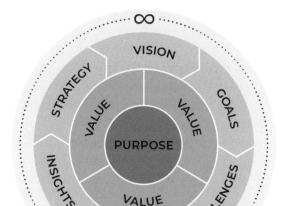

A 'Vision' generally reaches for the stars, which is a great starting point. Think of NASA's vision back in the 1960s of 'Putting a man on the moon.' It clearly states the ambition – but it does not say how to achieve it, let alone 'why' we should put a man on the moon. That comes later on.

'Goals' are more tangible and articulate what achieving success will mean. Make sure these are SMART (Specific, Measurable, Achievable, Realistic and Time-bound). For example: 'Build a rocket by the end of the year that can carry three people to the moon and back."

'Challenges' refers to the barriers and hurdles you have to overcome, including macro-constraints such as taxation, market access, strategic and operational issues such as cost, resource, building brand awareness, etc. For example: 'Low public awareness of the space program.'

Inside and outside 'Perceptions' are generally derived from active and passive market research, representing the voice of customers, employees and wider stakeholders. For example: 'Public perception is that there is no need to send a man to the moon.'

Insights distill Vision, Goals, Challenges and Perceptions into meaningful cornerstones to help shape Strategy. This step formulates the 'How to' in clear and actionable language. For example: 'Build positive public awareness for the space program.'

The second layer is where appropriate values are defined. This layer bridges the outer layer of 'how' to the inner-why, or Purpose. The best results are achieved by keeping the list of values to three to four important ones. Often two to three values describe a desired internal cultural behavior while one value clearly differentiates against competition. For example: 'Safety, Excellence and Exploration' – whereas 'Exploration' might serve as the differencing value.

It is important to come up with values that are as unique as possible and select the ones that keep your company relevant in the future. Certain attributes such as 'Integrity' and 'Trust' are appealing to everyone and therefore, so commonly used that they are no longer unique and differentiating. Equally, if everything is a core value, then nothing is really a priority. We will address how to discover distinct values a bit later on.

Starting a meaningful journey of Purpose transformation requires first asking what business you are in: is your value proposition clearly defined? If you are Harley-Davidson, are you in the business of building motorcycles or fulfilling dreams of personal freedom? One question is rational and limiting, while the other one is limitless and hard to put a price tag on. Are you clear on what you sell, how you source it, for whom it is and how you sell it? If the answer to these questions are either unclear or perhaps not clearly aligned internally, then it's a good idea to start creating a common understanding of the business you are in and how it works first, before moving on. A good starting point is to create a simple SWOT analysis. Slightly more elaborate yet still straight forward is using a visual open source framework designed by Alex Osterwalder, *The Business Model Canvas*.[136] These are simple enough and readily available tools to frame some of the questions around business direction.

We assume however, that at this point your actual offering, or your value proposition, is clear. Over time, we have been able to experience, test, experiment and synthesize what works best with brands, companies and individuals to guide them systematically from value proposition (business) to articulating who they really are. Crystallizing clarity requires to dig deeper and working through the *GPS Framework* layers outside in to start with. Circular rings indicate the layer of the *GPS Framework* you are currently working on. For ease of navigation, these can be found at the bottom right-hand corner on each of the following illustrations.

Strategy, Brand, Purpose

| Strategy | Brand | Purpose |

The outer ring of the *GPS Framework* helps us to put the business proposition into context. A linear description is helpful for this. The following diagram guides us in moving from Vision to desired Position. A ready-to-use template as well as examples are also available for download on the GPS website. The steps are exactly the same as described above. Simply state your vision and tangible goals – this space is your territory of opportunity. Clearly, there are challenges to overcome in order to achieve your vision and goals. List them under Challenges before moving on. What does the market think of you? What do internal and external stakeholders think? List these under the Perception section. If you don't have market studies or actual data available, consider creating your own insights and survey. We have developed a concise and powerful set of questions to help you structure this process. A sample questionnaire can be found for download on the GPS website in the framework section.

The Brand Strategy Map

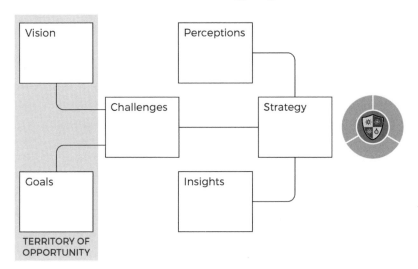

Moving inwards, we are now looking at the second layer of the *GPS Framework*. Whilst it is not our intent to deep dive into the language of Brand Management, we will briefly touch on it here in order to help you build an understanding of how Brand Definition works.

The Brand Framework

The Brand Core

Clearly marks the Brand Promise and positions the brand through differentiating core values in the hearts and minds of people.

Brand Strategy

Articulates how we 'deliver' the brand. The Brand Strategy is derived from the Brand Core and provides a 'how to' guide for consistent communications, which can be adjusted for respective channels and target groups.

Implementation (Product, Sales, Communication)

Internal and external audiences perceive the brand as 'relevant' and 'desirable.' The brand becomes the guiding instrument with which to shape and influence products and services, sales processes and communication both internally and externally.

Our goal here is to identify the values that best support the core. Values are used to describe a desired behavior and should be descriptive, unique and limited to no more than three or four. Each value can be articulated with words and images. Whilst it is easy to define internal values (think of 'trustworthy,' 'authentic,' etc.), at least one value should be tied to differentiation and directly reflect the desired position of the brand. Brand Value definition should not be taken lightly. Through either existing research or tailored surveys, an initial 'Value Cloud' can be produced to help shape the direction in which to look for suitable descriptors. Through a process of definition, refinement, testing and elimination, core values are evaluated and identified. It is important to note that core values should also be complementary to each other and be future proof. Values that hold true today might not be right for a business or a market space that is undergoing tremendous change. It therefore helps to quickly plot your values against the dimension of time and involvement.

Brand Value articulation takes the final set of core values and renders them tangible. For clarity and context, each of the Brand Values is supported by a short description in words as well as a key visual that underpins the desired effect of intuitive meaning.

Future-Proofing Brand Values

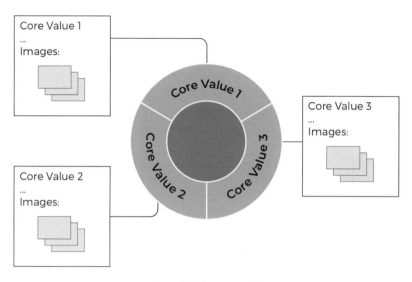

Brand Value Articulation

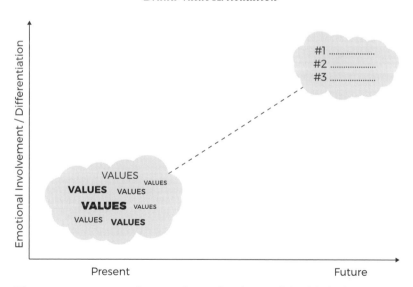

The appropriate articulation of Brand Values will build the backbone and architectural blueprint for creating the Brand Guidelines that will later bring your brand to life. If you are ready to deep dive further, please check the *GPS* website for further resources, ready-to-use frameworks, brand-value surveys, brand value books and tools to use in your work.

Seeking and Finding Purpose

"Logic will get you from A to B.
Imagination will take you everywhere."

Albert Einstein
German-born Theoretical Physicist

Because everyone has his or her own unique inner Purpose (consciously or not), it is best to explain the process of finding it by means of an example. Think about your fingerprints. The general pattern is fundamentally the same as that of billions of other people. There is not a person on our planet that has a fingerprint that is different in its *overall* design. However, at the same time, every fingerprint is absolutely unique. Understanding this is key to understanding the framework for discovering Purpose. Like your fingerprint, Purpose marks your unique identity with the same universal system.

Having a clear idea as to where we are going with our value proposition, what the strategy is, how we want to position ourselves and how we want to articulate our brand, we are now at the very core of our journey. *The GPS Framework* laid out the overarching Purpose as the inner core of three circular layers. Getting to the roots of Purpose is visualized as the inside of a capital V – V for 'Voluntas,' Latin for 'of good Purpose.'

Seeking & Finding Purpose

Intangible,
Open Thinking,
Detachment

Defining,
Clarifying,
Articulating

Sharpening
Purpose

Key Mind Shifting Questions

What's the secret of asking a question that
answers itself?
What are the right questions to ask to find out
the right questions to ask?
What question has never been asked about a
higher Purpose?
What is the optimum way of asking a question
about the inner Know-Why?
How do you ensure your values evolve in the
future and beyond?
What are the frameworks and rules that define a
good Purpose?
How do you crystallize your idea of who you are?
What is the best way to articulate Purpose?
Who are you? Where do you want to be?
And how do you get there?

Fundamental Exploratory Questions

What is the meaning of your brand?
What is it all about?
Who are we?
What is meaningful and valuable in life?
What is the significance of what we do?
What is the origin of our organization?
What is the nature of this institution?
What is the value of our journey?
What is the nature of reality?
What is our reason to exist?
What are we here for?
Why are we here?

The top part of the V represents freethinking, openly exploring intangible notions, wandering with curiosity in detachment from the world of limits and gravity. The middle part represents defining, clarifying and articulating. The bottom of the letter V denotes the method of zooming in on a singular, tangible Purpose. This process is systematic and holistic, moving from the intellectual to the practical. One must begin with the abstract and then venture downwards to the tangible. The process is driven by the need to adopt an outside-in perspective in order to be able to come up with a Purpose that radiates from the inside out.

It helps at this step to detach from the fast pace of everyday life and take an external viewpoint. This means escaping our daily routines to see the bigger picture. To be able to find our core Purpose, we must go against gravity and ascend high enough to gain a holistic view. This is difficult as there is a very powerful gravitational pull from the hot core of the earth – or in other words, our daily, operational tasks pull us back to the tangibility of milestones, deliverables and results. The laws of physics tell us that this force has the incredible energy to attract and pull everything to the center, keeping us in a constant gridlock. It is an indisputable *law*, but fortunately this is not a physical workout. Rather, this is a metaphysical exercise, so the laws are constituted in a different way. Whereas the pace of life will generally pull us back to rationality, this stage requires us to deliberately make time to detach. The direction is upward, not forward. It is an astral journey that broadens our thinking by dissolving conventional limits. "*Sic itur ad astra*" or "Thus one journeys to the stars" as the ancient Roman poet Virgil put it.

The mechanics for finding Purpose operates via systematic interactions. Reflecting on the following set of questions below will help stimulate the process of detached thinking.

Mind Framing Questions

What is truly transformational about your inner Know-Why?
How do you ensure your values evolve in the future and beyond?
How do you crystallize your idea of who you are?
Who are you? Where do you want to be?
And how do you get there?

Exploratory Questions

What is meaningful and valuable in life?
What is the significance of what we do?
What is the origin of our organization?
What is the nature of this institution?
What is the value of our journey?
What is the nature of reality?
What is our reason to exist?
What are we here for?
Why are we here?

Articulating and Clarifying Purpose

"The more original a discovery, the more obvious it seems afterwards."

Arthur Koestler, CBE
Hungarian–British Author and Journalist
Sonning Prize Laureate

What is the technique to articulating Purpose? How does one craft a good Purpose statement? Formulating such an important statement means finding the best way to communicate an organization's impact on the brand itself as well as the lives of its employees, customers, and surrounding community. We are now venturing down to the pointed edge of our letter V, where we start to solidify our Purpose by refining it with language.

This is the part where the skills of a wordsmith comes into play. A careful choice of words steers us away from falling into the trap of short-lived clichés. All words with highly negative connotations; denotations, implications, associations and indications need to be eliminated right away. If you are not in the advertising, fashion, design or any other creative industry you might not be aware of extremely overused buzzwords. It is important to stay clear of these, so that you don't end up with a corny Purpose statement such as: "To make the world a better place." It is also important that you consider the subjectivity of your Purpose statement. What sounds good to you may seem too abstract and vague for the people in your organization to grasp it and make it actionable.

The entire operation of articulating and formulating Purpose is a very delicate process. We need the 'oenologist' to handpick every single word with meticulous care and with utmost concentration. Word formulation must be more descriptive than prescriptive, stating who and why you exist, rather than what you do. If you are not being absolutely honest with yourself and if the element of intrinsic sincerity is absent, then you might miss the point. Apart from being clearly understood, your statement must be *instantly felt*.

A good Purpose statement must work intrinsically from within and should allow for connection. It is not a vision or multi-paragraph mission statement that needs to be memorized, but rather a combination of minimal words that maximize meaning. Putting your statement through a 'filter' can help you fine-tune its power.

Checklist for a good Purpose statement ...

- Ideally starts with an action word (verb) that evokes a sense of movement

- Provides deeper meaning for a brands ecosystem

- Requires context that renders it universal yet unique

- Expresses the overarching 'Reason Why' by relating to what you do

- Is always true from within and a demonstration of utmost integrity

- Connects with the head and the heart, speaking to both rational and emotional needs

- Remains short, simple and memorable in ideally no more than five words

An issue that frequently arises when crafting Purpose statements is the confusion around 'Purpose' and 'Strapline, Slogan or Claim'. Particularly for non-brand executives, the distinction is too subtle to be intuitive. Both are short and powerful. Both are engaging. Yet they serve very different reasons.

A strapline is often descriptive in nature at the inception of a brand and evolves over time to an elevated, intrinsic expression (i.e. think of Apple's 'Think Different' or Harley-Davidson's 'Live Your Legend'[137]). A Strapline is catchy, often tied to a particular campaign and serves to differentiate for determined period of time. When a company or a product is young and does not have the broad consumer awareness, straplines most often are 'descriptive,' i.e. they tie the name to a clear value proposition. As awareness builds and a company and brand mature, straplines often help to build stronger, emotional connections. Look at the abbreviated list of Coca-Cola's straplines[138] over time for illustration:

Coca-Cola Strapline Evolution

Year	Strapline
1900	For headache and exhaustion, drink Coca-Cola
1939	Thirst asks Nothing More
1952	What you want is a Coke
1969	It's the Real Thing
1985	Americas Real Choice
2000	Coca-Cola. Enjoy
2009	Open Happiness
2016 present	Taste the Feeling

In reality, Coco-Cola's strapline changed over 60 times in between its inception in 1886–2016. What changes less frequently is a brands identity. Again, let's take a look at Coca-Cola and its respective evolution of identity:

Coca-Cola Identity Evolution

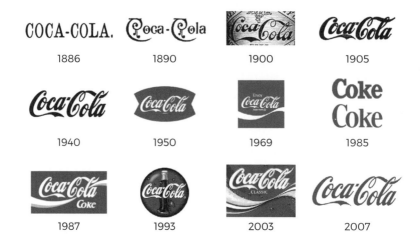

It is interesting to note that brands change both straplines and identities to adjust not just with consumers and their relative degree of brand/product awareness, but reflect broader shifts in times and society overall in order to create relevancy.

A Purpose statement, on the other hand, is only truly intuitive and meaningful when understood in context, serving as the all-encompassing, philosophical canvas that provides long-term guidance and direction. Thy reflect an overarching philosophy that provides near unwavering direction. It is a lot less subject to economic or societal cycles and ideally holds over time. Whilst slogans can change every other year, an identity every five to ten years, an overarching Purpose often remains unchanged for a half century or more. IKEA's Purpose statement of 'Creating a better everyday life for the many people' for instance remains unaffected despite the rapid evolution of distribution channels, the fast pace of technological and fashion cycles in home furniture etc. The core ideology remains the same.

The dynamic and fundamental difference between a strapline (or positioning claim) and the unwavering spiritual canvas a genuine Purpose statement can provide is perhaps best illustrated by looking at Apple.

Case in Point: Apple

Steve Jobs had a vision: 'To make a contribution to the world by making tools for the mind that advance humankind.'[139] Apple does not operate according to a typical outside-in model, but rather adopts an inside-out approach, combining technology with aesthetics in new and innovative ways. With this approach, it inspires and attracts future talent who believe in making a difference for the sake of mankind, rather than simply churning out the next best gadget. Steve Jobs was obsessed with making things intuitive, safe and easy for us humble humans to use. Apple's overarching Purpose statement can aptly be summarized as 'Humanizing Technology' – two powerful words, loaded with meaning when understood in context. And with it, Steve Jobs proved to the world that the complexity of technology could coexist in harmony with aesthetic simplicity. Apple's ensuing breakthrough strapline 'Think Different' appealed to the creative minds, setting Apple apart from its PC rivals.

Note Apple's current mission statement:

'Apple designs Macs, the best personal computers in the world, along with OS X, iLife, iWork and professional software. Apple leads the digital music revolution with its iPods and iTunes online store. Apple has reinvented the mobile phone with its revolutionary iPhone and App store and is defining the future of mobile media and computing devices with iPad.'

Clearly, Apple is a much larger company today than back in the days when a small team of geeks gave every bit of their energy to change the world. One can argue that mission statements change over time and that as companies grow, they become more 'hands on.' However, Purpose endures. Apple is still in the business of 'Humanizing Technology.'

As Steven Pinker, a cognitive scientist, states in his book *The Sense of Style*: "Governments and corporations have found that small improvements in clarity can prevent vast amounts of error, frustration, and waste..."[140] It isn't incidental that in our age of clutter, the number one bestseller on Amazon (selling over two million copies) is a book about the Japanese art of decluttering and organizing.[141] The more clutter there is in our minds, the more difficult it is to clearly articulate a Purpose statement. Managing increasing complexity is about having the skills to condense and compress your deepest, most inner beliefs into universal meaningfulness.

Purpose Articulation

Purpose Checklist

· Simple
· Contextual
· True from within
· Connects with the head and the heart
· Serves as an overarching reason why
· Is closer than you think
  (universal, yet tangible)

Purpose Statement

ACTION WORD (VERB) + ATTRIBUTE (WHAT) = 5 WORDS OR LESS

If vision is where you are going, the brand an expression of who you are, and strategy how you get there, then Purpose is *why* you do what you do. The *GPS Framework* helps translate the intrinsic nature of Purpose into something tangible that eventually evolves into an empowering thrust from within. The aim is to maintain universal meaning easy enough to grasp. In the words of the French political writer Francois Gautier: "More important than the quest for certainty is the quest for clarity."

Shared and Aligned Purpose

"If two things are equal to the same thing,
they are equal to each other."

Euclid of Alexandria
Father of Geometry

A powerful and well-functioning Purpose aligns vertically as well as horizontally. In other words, it is shared and aligned within a brand's ecosystem.

Here is a good test for you to try. Take a minute and answer the following questions:

1. What is your Purpose? Can you articulate your answer in five words or less?

2. Now ask your peers, colleagues and boss: What is our Purpose? Can they articulate this in five words or less? If their answer is coherent with your answer to question 1, then you can rejoice in claiming 'shared Purpose.'

3. To gain an external perspective, ask your customers, suppliers and business partners: What do we stand for and what is our Purpose? If they give you the same answer (in meaning, rather than in exact words) as your internal colleagues, you can nudge up and claim 'aligned Purpose.'

It is very rare for people to achieve cohesion on these three simple questions. Most people cannot even articulate an answer to the first question, let alone claim full coherence on questions two and three.

If you answered all three questions with ease, this is the place to stop reading. Skip this chapter (or most of this book, in fact) and work on your strategy of 'how' to make things happen.

Shared & Aligned Purpose

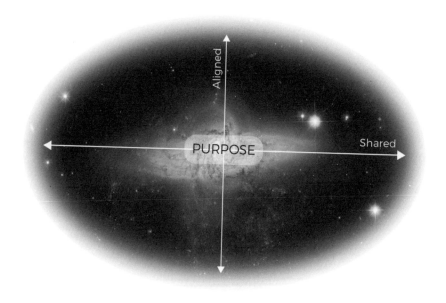

Creating shared and aligned Purpose is not as easy as the above test implies. It requires deep thinking and engagement on a cultural level. The process of 'soul-searching' to find Purpose is often triggered by a necessary market alignment, a repositioning, a need for change, rapid growth etc.

Research conducted by the American Management Association revealed that in organizations with more than 1000 employees, 61% of respondents considered staff to be less loyal now, compared to ten years ago.[142] Low morale was the most commonly identified consequence of decreasing loyalty (84%), followed by high turnover and disengagement

(80%), growing distrust amongst colleagues (76%), and lack of team spirit (73%).[143]

These are disturbing figures. Yet, when we ask directors, managers and executives, "What is your company's most valuable asset?" they reply with a cliché: "Our people." However, this is sadly flawed because firstly, people are not 'assets' and secondly, people come and go. Your brand is the only thing that stays. It embodies every aspect of your company, including your people. Earlier we discussed the power of brand and that if managed carefully and consistently, it can create tremendous value over time.

Professor Chris Roebuck, a British economist who advises top organizations on maximizing performance through effective leadership, asked Markus Kramer, then Aston Martin's CMO about the company's Customer Relationship Management system in order to better understand the link between CRM and effective leadership. The answer was as unexpected as it was candid, "We don't have one – yet it works." In other words, successful relationship management is not only about the system, the infrastructure or technology, it is first and foremost about the internal mindset that lies at the heart of an organization's culture. The catalyst of the mindset, the guiding compass and the path to an interconnected culture is rooted in the brand's inner Purpose. Technology certainly adds value in terms of empowering people with tools and information, but it can't replace a deeply ingrained Purpose that radiates from within. If shared and aligned internally and externally, Purpose has the power to unleash the type of passion, cohesion and consistency no CRM system has yet managed to replicate.

A Purpose-driven brand becomes the passing torch of enthusiasm and passion of *why* you do what you do. One of the key responsibilities of marketing leaders today then, other than making sure short-term targets are hit, is to facilitate and distribute the glue that builds and holds a brand together for the long-term.

In order to make these frameworks more tangible, let's take a look at a real-life example. For illustrative purposes, we chose to pick a company at its inception.

Case in Point: P1 Graphene Solutions

2D Technology is a Startup based in London and New York taking advantage of science and technology in the rapidly evolving world of wonder materials. Graphene makes things stronger; it's the most resistant and impermeable membrane ever. It's 200x stronger and 6x lighter than steel, extremely thin, transparent and bendable. It's also faster; electron mobility is 70x higher than in silicon and conducts heat 10x better than copper.

A key issue in this market is the sheer limitless opportunities the coming graphene revolution promises. Starting with the Business Model Canvas, the Startup decided to focus its efforts on translating the 'mad graphene science' into actionable traction for the motorsports and high-end car segment first, before branching out into other transport related fields – and consequently also 'adjusted' its still young name to P1 Graphene Solutions. Today, P1 Graphene is in the business of creating custom solutions for the application of graphene within the automotive sector. Specifically, this results in lower vehicle weight, less emissions and improved fuel efficiency.

Working through the outer ring of the *GPS Framework*, we first firm up the company's vision and its goals, identifying its territory of opportunity. From there we work through the challenges to overcome, we look at perceptions, derive insights and formulate a strategic direction leading to a desired future. P1 Graphene's bold vision is '*To take Graphene from Cars to Mars.*'

Moving one layer inside the *GPS Framework* requires us to think through P1 Graphene's value system. Which values will drive the desired behavior in the future, which ones can help differentiate the company in an industry that is mostly driven by scientists? Articulating the companies value system resulted in the following core values: *Pioneering, Collaborative and Focused.*

So then, what is P1 Graphene's raison d'être? We first come back to our Purpose statement checklist: keep it short and simple, ideally start with an action word, provide deeper meaning, make it contextual and make it true from within, – all ideally expressed in no more than five words. This is the point where we need to detach from the tangible work we've done so far. This is also the moment where individual reflection is needed before the power of collective alignment can produce a suitable shared and aligned Purpose statement.

In practical terms, it helps to simply hand out post-it notes, pull up some of the mind-shifting and exploratory questions of the V-formula and ask people to reflect, think and articulate possible Purpose statements – individually, one per Post-it. Simply grouping the Purpose Post-its allows us to cluster the collective thinking. Sure, you will have to separate 'strapline' thinking from the deeper reflections pointing towards the inner Know-Why, but that's a relatively easy exercise. You can't expect a final product either, but it will get you about 80% there – no need for lengthy year-long thinking retreats and countless brainstorms causing more confusion than clarity. The remaining 20% of effort is about going through the Purpose statement checklist and articulating supporting context.

P1 Graphene's Purpose statement is: *Positively Transforming Performance.* Just three words sum up the positive impact on materials, people, processes and the output that ultimately benefits clients and the world at large. P1 Graphene's Purpose statement describes more than the way the company does things. It describes who they are and *why* they do what they do.

The following section demonstrates in short and visual succession, how we can move from 'an idea' to a well thought through and articulated brand proposition using the *GPS Framework* and methodology presented thus far. Please also make sure to watch the explaining video and feel free to download all frameworks at www.guidingpurposestrategy.com.

Case in Point: XSPACE

XSpace is a new business entering the US market with innovative storage solutions for professionals, personal users and investors. It taps into the wave of aging demographics and is for people who look to right-size their housing needs in the coming decades. The value proposition elevates the existing offering of self-storage to entirely new levels. An initial flagship project is planned in Austin Texas. A quick build and turn-around by 2020 will mean a steep learning curve and a parallel opportunity to start scaling to 100+ projects across the US rapidly.

The following illustrations demonstrate the 'real life working' application of the *GPS Framework* when embedded into a brand development process in a visual and tangible way.

The Brand Model Development Process

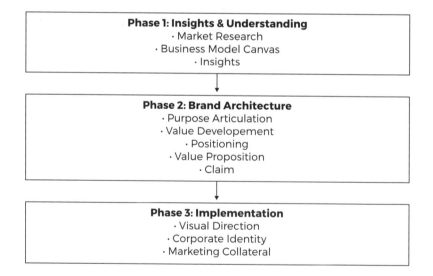

Phase 1 – Insights & Understanding

Insights through quantitative and qualitative research, competitive review, business model and frameworks are brought together in a clearly defined, well-structured workshop aligning understanding and direction for all stakeholders. All *GPS Framework* documents are worked through sequentially and for the basis for clarity in articulating the 'brand to be.'

195

Phase 2 – Brand Architecture

Distilling all input into a coherent, value-based brand model. Whilst we work from the 'outside in' during the workshop, this phase consists of re-constructing the developed brand from the inside out.

Business Model Canvas Outcome

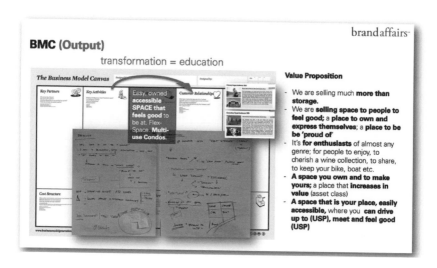

Positioning Outcome

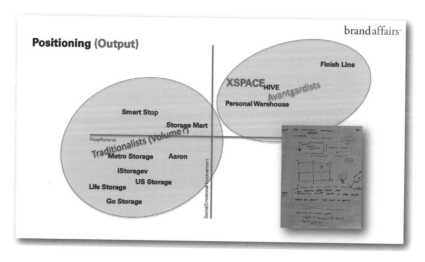

Strategy Map Outcome

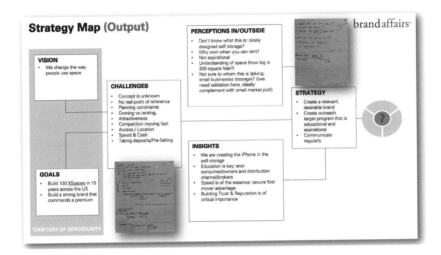

Values Outcome

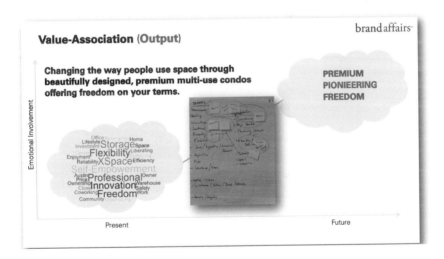

Purpose Outcome

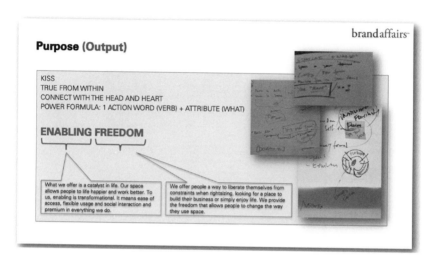

Brand Model Development

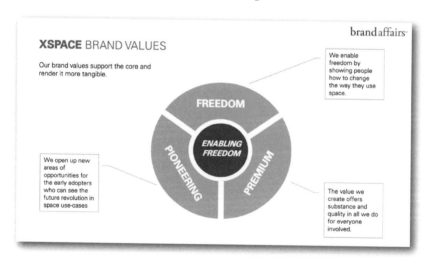

Purpose Articulation

XSPACE PURPOSE

brand affairs™

ENABLING FREEDOM

What we offer is pioneering in spirit and represents a catalyst in life. Our space allows people to live happier and work better. To us, enabling is transformational. It means ease of access, flexible usage and social interaction. Premium in everything we do. We offer people a way to liberate themselves from constraints when rightsizing, looking for a place to build their business, scale their investments or simply enjoy life. **We enable freedom by showing people how to change the way they use space.**

Claim Development

XSPACE

brand affairs™

XSPACE

make it your place

Phase 3 – Implementation

The objective of the brand work is to have a long-lasting effect on the future of XSpace and hence should be both embedded with momentum at the beginning where tangible output is easiest to achieve and on an on-going basis where the brand will drive consistency of values and a 'common language'. This phase is therefore all about the successful implementation of the jointly developed brand model and its resulting measures across the business.

Visual Design Development

Defining Corporate Identity

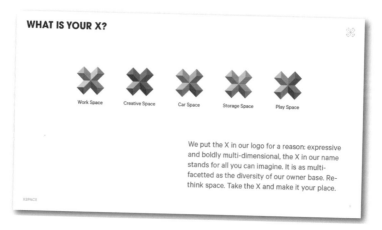

Developing Copy

Touch-Point Application & Collateral

Measuring Purpose

*"Measure what is measurable,
and make measurable what is not so."*

Galileo Galilei
Italian Mathematician and Physician

Something nonexistent starts to exist the moment we measure it. Today, quantum physicists can explain through mathematical measurements how something is. We have all had our first experiences with measuring starting back in elementary school. How could we ever forget our first ruler? The word 'ruler' also means the sovereign or the supreme authority that defines the rules to run an establishment, a tribe or a nation. We tend to forget that there is an intimate relationship between the capability to rule and the ability to measure.

It is helpful to bear in mind that identifying *what* is to be measured is as crucial as knowing how it will be measured. While the role of measuring is very important in the realm of business, it is often misunderstood. The luxury industry adopts an interesting approach to measuring success. Unlike many other industries, luxury companies don't measure success by how many products they sell. And when it comes to brand communication strategies, success is not measured by how many consumers have seen an advertisement or read a promotional message.

The luxury industry considers the *who*, not the 'how many' as a significant indicator of success. Or in other words, measurement is based on quality, not quantity. Dr William Edwards Deming created the concept of Total Quality Management (TQM). It was this very concept that put postwar Japan on the map of the most powerful economies in the world. Despite being a statistician, Deming believed that "The most important things cannot be measured." With regards to long-term values, strategy and vision, quantity is almost always prioritized over quality in all sectors except the luxury sector. Case in point – *quam bene non quantum* (quality over quantity) is the motto we suggest for success in the 21st century.

Measuring Purpose within a company's culture requires establishing whether Purpose can maintain its position of relevance. If not, values need to be adjusted to match the inner Purpose. In order to test and verify if Purpose is still shared and aligned within your organization, leaders must cultivate an open dialogue with their employees, suppliers, customers and extended stakeholders.

Like consumer loyalty, employee loyalty needs to be built over time. Branding and social media specialist Simon Mainwaring says: "Ensure your employees understand what your brand stands for so they can be your first line of word-of-mouth advertising." Satisfied Purpose-oriented employees are nearly 50% more likely to promote their employer externally[144]. Hence, accessing the viral spiral applies not only to B2C and B2B communication, but it also works at the employee level. It is therefore wise to give employees something worthwhile to engage in. Ensuring the culture and values of your company remain alive, motivational and inspirational is a good place to start.

According to a Deloitte survey, 73% of employees who say they work in a Purpose-oriented company are engaged, compared to 23% of those who don't.[145] Implementing Purpose reviews are therefore just as important as performance reviews. Measuring Purpose helps to understand if people are fully engaged and feel part of the bigger picture, inside and outside of the organization.

There are, of course, several challenges in measuring Purpose. From our conversations with various Purpose-driven organizations, we identified two main problems with measuring Purpose. One problem is that such surveys are not done on a regular basis. Companies would have a better reflection of their internal cultures if employee surveys were more frequently conducted. The length of 'culture' surveys is another issue. When a survey is too long participants are less likely to be consistent in the way they answer questions. Similar to measuring Net Promoter Score (NPS, used as a proxy to determine customer satisfaction and loyalty based on likelihood of recommendation), we suggest reducing Purpose measurement to a single question.

We believe that the *Purpose Review Metric* (PRM) question does the trick. This simple question works because it uniquely measures internal culture components that are directly related to an employee's experience and journey within the organization. The PRM question is measured on a simple ten-point scale and is constructed as follows:

"How inclined are you to recommend your employer to those closest to you, i.e., family, best friends, relatives, etc.?"

Purpose Review Metric

Not Inclined								Inclined	
1	2	3	4	5	6	7	8	9	10
Ineffective / Low cohesion				Neutral				Shared	

Admittedly simple, we come to the conclusion that this single question has the power to elicit the sincerest answers possible. At once the answer to this question offers an indicator of likely performance, discretionary effort, integrity, transparency, clarity and, ultimately, growth. In aggregate, it measures the level of *shared* Purpose within a company's culture and is an indicator how well it is aligned within its broader ecosystem – in particular when contrasted against NPS. If you don't measure NPS in your business, then the question above can simply be replicated outside your business to measure 'aligned' Purpose.

"How inclined are you to recommend [company X] to those closest to you, i.e., family, best friends, relatives, etc.?"

The ultimate goal is to score high in both employee happiness and customer satisfaction. PRM is efficient and works best if asked anonymously and at regular intervals. Forward-thinking companies are acutely aware that measuring shared and aligned Purpose is critical. In fact, Deming claimed that a lack of loyalty toward Purpose is among the top five deadly diseases of American businesses. Customers won't be loyal to your brand so long as you are not loyal to your brands overarching Purpose. It goes without saying that this does not only concern American businesses, but companies all around the globe.

Key Performance Indicators (KPIs) for brands, corporations and organizations vary. What they have in common is an alignment with the fundamental goals of what makes a business a business. KPI measurements (which, in this context, includes PRM) are crucial for continued success and should be aligned with *The Guiding Purpose Strategy* at all times.

Five Purpose-oriented KPIs

1. **PRM** - Purpose Review Metric, measuring 'Shared Purpose' within an organization

2. **NPS** - Net Promoter Score, measuring external satisfaction, loyalty and retention, can serve as a proxy for measuring 'Aligned Purpose' within the extended value chain

3. **CAR** - Customer Acquisition Ratio (% of new customers), as an indicator for continued growth

4. **MS** – Market Share (% of market), as a benchmark against competition

5. **EBIT** – Earnings Before Interest & Taxes (operational profit), measuring economic viability

There is a fine line between measuring for the sake of measuring and measuring to manage. If we are to create a better world, then our measurement must take Purpose into account. Or in the words of Bill Gates: "I have been struck again and again by how important measurement is to improve the human condition."

Purpose in Times of Crisis

"In crises, the most daring course is often safest."

Dr. Henry Kissinger
American politician, diplomat, and geopolitical consultant

The clarity of one's reason for being makes for a steadfast pole, especially in times of change and ambiguity, helping us to weather economic and personal ups and downs that life throws at us. In this sense, Purpose becomes a very reliable, if not the only one, core during tormented times. It provides a source of certainty in the midst of uncertainty. It is perhaps the best, if not the only, provider of clarity.

It helps to recall that the still point of our spinning planet is the North Star. That gleaming object that the rest of the heavens appear to move around. Steadfast, in the same location every night from dusk to dawn, neither rising nor setting, providing unwavering guidance when we look to the skies – and perhaps beyond. So then, what should we look out for to successfully navigate choppy times for our businesses, brands and our teams?

Unless you just drive for the fun of it, you will very likely have a destination to reach in mind. Imagine you take a wrong turn, then your GPS simply says: "Recalculating Route". Your GPS doesn't turn off or cancel your route. It simply says 'recalculating' - and keeps venturing forward, making sure you reach your destination as smooth and fast as possible. It re-aligns your intention with the current context in mind. For businesses, this means to re-align while strengthening the core. It is a way of evolving while not negotiating the core from which one leads. This is a delicate balance between consistency and relevance. It is important to remember that going in-sync with the turbulent times must not stop brands from staying true to their brand Purpose. Balancing the *diachronic* identity for consistency with the *synchronic* situation for relevance is key. Keeping one's integrity is the priority of all priorities. The force stays with those who are clear on their Know-Why and combine this with strategic maneuverability.

Communication has always played a big role in many types of crises throughout history. Both interpersonal and public communication are of interest here. Curating the right words is especially important during the time of crisis. Words can function as tools for framing, choice creation and navigational direction. Moreover, language is the mirror of culture whether it is the culture of a country, city, industry, discipline or a brand. As Dr. Sigmund Freud pointed out: "Words and magic were in the beginning one and the same thing, and even today words retain much of their magical power."[146] The right words can spark actions, create movements, reduce uncertainty, maximize social cohesion, facilitate calm and stimulate the economy.

No matter how uncertain, any crisis is temporary. What one does right in the short-term will have a positive return in the long-term. So instead of being stuck in the short-term reality, it is important to see the bigger picture. Only those that look beyond immediate situations are those who see a broader plethora of possibilities. As the Nobel laureate, Dr. Daniel Kahneman wisely advised, long-term decisions need to be made with slow thinking.[147] But without safety, it is difficult to envisage the future. How can leaders provide a sense of safety in a situation of uncertainty?

It is especially during crisis that leaders who adopt a long-term perspective enjoy a better perceived reputation. The opposite then should hold true of course, too. For example, during the 2008 financial crisis and its subsequent recession, businesses that lowered or paused their marketing activities regretted it later. Those who decide to retract marketing budgets during a crisis are likely to experience detrimental effects, even 3-5 years post economic recovery.[148] As Mark Ritson, brand consultant and former marketing professor, noted: "companies that increased their ad budgets during the recession grew sales much faster than their rivals – not only during the downturn but also beyond it. Companies that decreased their advertising spend saw their sales decline both during the recession and then for the following three years. (…) Despite studying different firms across very different recessions, each study revealed that maintaining or even increasing ad spend during a downturn is invariably the right thing to do because it sets a company up to survive the downturn (a little) and then prosper (a lot) in the period that follows."[149] According to another study published in the Harvard Business Review: "Building and maintaining strong brands - ones that customers recognize and trust - remains one of the best ways to reduce business risk. The stock prices of companies with strong brands, such as Colgate-Palmolive and Johnson & Johnson, have held up better in recessions than those of large consumer product companies with less well-known brands."[150]

In times of instability, there is a stronger need for leadership. Purpose-oriented leaders take responsibility. Max DePree, the founder of Herman Miller, once said: "The first responsibility of a leader is to define reality." Responsibility is quite literally the ability to respond. One always has a choice on how to respond to a crisis. A well-rounded picture of the situation is therefore not just a matter of rational optimism, but also of analytical realism so that the ground for action can be prepared. All the promises we've made as leaders or as leading brands are being put to the test in a period of crisis. As Denis Leary said: "Crisis doesn't create character. It reveals it." So, it is in a moment of turmoil that much of an organization's persona is revealed.

The pandemic COVID-19 crisis in 2020 made people and organizations more crisis-conscious than ever on a transnational level. Instead of identifying problems, speaking of cancellations and delays along with other weaknesses from the economic impact of the virus impacting everyone, Purpose-oriented leaders directed their attention to strengths, possibilities, and solutions. They were quick with the facts and slow with the blame. For example, they spotted what cannot be canceled (independent strategic projects and personal passions). They made the best of the new free time born out of a crisis – and got the things done that couldn't be done when they didn't have the time. They identified the spheres that were either less affected or were thriving during this economic turmoil. Examples abound from ed-tech, health and pharma, teleworking, e-commerce, media (news, show business, digital apps, gaming, etc.) and many more.

Purpose-oriented individuals or organizations view a crisis as a decisive moment to strengthen one's core and work towards a strong emergence post crisis. Metaphorically speaking, when in crisis such individuals choose ecdysis – shedding of their old skin to allow for renewal and for further growth. They see opportunities where everybody else sees problems and, more importantly, they are able to focus exclusively on exploiting those opportunities.

In what ways can almost any type of crisis be reframed as an opportunity?

- It is an opportunity to be creative

- It is an opportunity for re-alignment or even reinvention

- It is an opportunity to invest in one's organization

- It is an opportunity to invest in your identity and your brand

- It is an opportunity to invest in personal advancement

Winners have an optimistic mindset. They see opportunities where everybody else sees problems and, more importantly, they are able to focus exclusively on exploiting those opportunities.

As the saying goes: every cloud has a silver lining. It is a truism that after every crisis, big changes and paradigm shifts shape our future. This can be a shift into a new economic realm, a new sociological milieu or a novel world order. Authority is needed during and after such shifts. The value of 'prophets and idols' with freewill and goodwill rises during times of uncertainty and we look 'up to our leaders', may these be political, entrepreneurial or spiritual. Whether it is being a clear voice in a sea of noise or delivering independent thinking, it is, first of all, leadership that is expected to know where we all need to go (à la "the man with the plan") that we look to. In other words:

good crisis management is also, and perhaps first and foremost, about strong leadership based on taking responsibility and initiative. It is therefore sensible to put genuine, Purpose driven thinking at the heart of our thinking.

Applying Purpose

Position to Be First

"Don't try to make a product for everybody,
because that is a product for nobody.
The everybody products are all taken."

Seth Godin
Entrepreneur, Marketing Guru and Writer

In July 1969, Neil Armstrong was the first human being to set foot on the moon. Edwin 'Buzz' Aldrin followed only minutes later, while Michael Collins kept steering Apollo 11 in the moon's orbit. Most of us know of Neil Armstrong. Few of us remember Buzz Aldrin. No one recalls Michael Collins, although without him the mission could not have been completed – neither Neil Armstrong nor Buzz Aldrin could have made it back to planet earth. The point here is that if you position yourself or your business, then only being first really works. Positioning is about occupying a certain space in someone else's mind. If you can't be first, rethink your strategy.

You can't be the second Facebook or the next Google. Copying them will not take you anywhere new. Notice that neither Facebook or Google articulated their Purpose so they could become large, cool or profitable – taking this road will surely misguide an entrepreneur's journey. Inspired by the need for dealing with the data-complexity of the future, Google's Purpose to 'Organize the World's Information' gave the company the thrust and energy to create something new.

There were several search engines before Google (Yahoo, Altavista, Lycos to name a few), and it would be wrong to say that they were the first to occupy the search space. The key characteristics of Google's invention lay in two strategic areas: technology and psychology. It was the first search engine that exclusively focused on the idea of searching. Other search engines displayed information in one big visual clutter, while Google offered one empty search box in the middle of an otherwise white screen. This aesthetic element stemmed from their psychological strategy. Internet users around the world trusted Google Search simply because it did *just that*: search the web.

Facebook's original intention was not to target the masses. It wasn't the first social network either. Still, it didn't copy the business models of similar networks. Although Facebook wasn't a luxury brand, it began its journey in the top segments, operating first in one of the most elite universities in the US, before spreading to other Ivy League colleges. Gradually, it trickled down to other colleges. It then went from students to younger internet users and from there, it conquered businesses and organizations around the globe. The key distinction in Facebook's brand management strategy was the fact that it began from the top of the pyramid, a distinction that created aspiration for the brand. The moral of the story: it is best never to aspire to be what already exists. There is no originality in becoming the second Coca-Cola.

Dave Higgins, consulting marketing director for Deloitte, said: "Senior executives in business have grown tired of overpromising and underdelivering and following the do-everything approach, like the famous German *Eierlegende Wollmilchsau* – ('egg-laying-wool-milk-giving-pig') – vainly trying to do everything for everyone."[166]

Luxury brands are extremely good at positioning. At a macro level, products in this category are not targeted at everyone to start with. Deliberate eliminators such as price or access exclude the vast majority of people. Luxury watches priced at $10,000 or above only attract a select group of watch collectors, status-seeking consumers or the 0.1% of the world's population for whom any amount of money is just no issue. Within such a tight, yet competitive market space, positioning is everything. Indeed, it triggers extreme effort on the part of companies seeking to carve out a niche. Take the Hublot "Big Bang $5 million" for example. It is not only a watch adorned with 1200 stunning diamonds (and costs, as the name indicates, five million), it is also a watch that clearly makes a very bold statement. The Hublot brand is assertive and bold in its positioning, clearly this is not a watch for everybody – even if you have the money. But for the right few, it is just the perfect match.

Integration

"Meaning leads to profits, not vice versa."

Stuart Crainer and Des Dearlove
British Management Journalists and Business Theorists

Application Programming Interfaces (APIs) help us integrate quicker and with less friction. If you are a traditional taxi driver, travel agency, hotel, bookseller or asset manager you probably already know what it feels like to live in a 'post-API' world. APIs increasingly connect the world of products and services with the end-consumer without anyone or anything in the middle. This is what is disrupting traditional value chains is all about and fuels the hope of future returns: the assumption that large parts of the middle will be cut out.

A post-API world offers few strategic choices: either you scale and become so large that you can survive with ever-thinner margins, or you differentiate and specialize. Whichever strategic context works better for you, consumers will be less forgiving of imperfect products or brands that overpromise and underdeliver. It is quite Darwinian. The smarter and stronger will survive while the weaker are driven into extinction by an omni-connected consumer.

The golden nugget is to create such a strong position in the hearts and minds of your customers that they will love you no matter what. Brands like

Harley-Davidson have mastered this feat: the brand has become synonymous with delivering on the promise of life as a journey, including every bit of adventure that goes with it. However, if you were an executive at Harley-Davidson Motor Company in the mid-1920s, you would probably have had quite a different perspective on the future. You would have been stuck in the middle, watching consumers satisfy their needs of transportation with pretty much anything else but a motorcycle. In a sense, Harley was quickly becoming a post-API player of its day.

Harley's strategic choice to escape the middle in the early '30s was powerful, yet pragmatic. The management took a bold decision and positioned the brand in the space of spending leisure time away from home or work, rather than a means of getting there. This simple idea has worked brilliantly – Harley-Davidson and is still going strong. Other companies have started adopting this concept, too. Think of Starbucks for example: a great place to socialize, meet people and feel good; or plug in and work for a couple of hours. Not your home, not your office either – it is your third place in a post-API environment.

Today more than ever, a brand has a direct link to what is on offer and who buys it (or not) simply because there is less of a buffer. No car dealer is responsible for the defects of your Hyundai, no concierge can butter you up when the room you booked through Airbnb is not quite what you expected. As a brand, you are responsible for the promise and the delivery. Purpose is the glue that holds your brand – staff, suppliers and customers included – together. Creating an integrated place where everyone in your brand's ecosystem can meet and feel well (physically and mentally) has the potential to give your brand legendary status and yield long-term benefits beyond your wildest imagination.

The following two chapters are kind contributions by Lilian Roten, Vice President Brand Management Swissôtel and Pullman as well as Julie Vice President Communications at KAYAK. These are two case in point stories that help demonstrate how granular integration needs to be for all touchpoints to work together. These are also great examples that demonstrate how transformational – and powerful – Purpose-driven brand activation can work.

Celebrating Purpose at Swissôtel

"The positive experience we create for our guests is deeply rooted in the understanding and appreciation for our environment, our people and our planet. Sustainable management means growth that doesn't cost the earth — because we are all guests of the world."

Lilian Roten
Contributing Author, Vice President
Brand Management Swissôtel and Pullman

Case in Point: Swissôtel

Over the decades, Swissôtel's role in the world has grown, driven by our commitment to our purpose and the values that we live every single day. That the brand did not only survive, but indeed thrived during turbulent times, weathering economic swings and multiple ownership changes, is a testimony to the strength of the brand. The journey ahead is an exciting one: 2020 marks 40 years of Swissôtel, making it the perfect time to celebrate our global citizenship and share the story of our brand. It is also an excellent time to reflect and share and pass on what makes us strong:

Clarity of Purpose
Our Purpose is 'Bringing Quality in Life'. While proud of our solid business performance, this is about celebrating our calling. Our Purpose

at Swissôtel is to make people feel taken care of and safe. We provide our guests and colleagues the peace of mind they need to recharge and enjoy their quality time, explore the world and discover life's true rewards.

Global Mindset

Swissôtel was founded in 1980 and born global. It is remarkable how our brand still shapes the way we do business today. While all other major competitors focused their growth on one country to start with and then slowly ventured out into the world, Swissôtel took a more global approach from the beginning. From the outset, we celebrated our Swiss heritage, were mindful of different cultures and customs, and knew that investment in excellent multilingual communication was key to our growth. Ultimately, we must continue to listen to the needs and wants of our global network to succeed.

Values: Heritage to Shape the Future

When shaping our product and service concepts, we continue to honor our Swiss roots and our belief in quality, efficiency and care. This includes our Pürovel Spa & Sport concept, a Swiss-inspired solution to healthy living. The Alpine seasons inform the concept's philosophy and mirror the four stages of natural vitality: renewal (spring) peak activity (summer), recovery (autumn), hibernation (winter).

Honing our values took us three decades and revolve around the Swissôtel brand passions: Vitality for Body and Mind, Sustainable Excellence and High-Quality Craftsmanship.

Positioning: Vitality for Body and Mind

Discovering one's values is a journey. For example, we initially used the word vitality when describing a guest spa treatment. It didn't take us long to realize that the essence of vitality resonated globally, even if there were slightly different interpretations around the world. In Asia, people viewed it as finding balance. In the USA, people associated vitality with aiming for more energy; while in Europe it implied feeling healthier. We believe in the power of Vitality as the origin of well-being. More than just a program, 'Vitality for body and mind' is a philosophy that focuses on enabling quality of life for our guests and colleagues. It is at the heart of everything we do.

Product and Innovation Swiss Style

We offer products and services designed to stimulate our guests' physical and mental fitness in their own time and comfort zone. Our Vitality Destination Walks help guests get fresh air and feel great while taking in the local sites. The Vitality coffee breaks for meeting attendees ensure the right type of nutritious food is served at the right time. While, our Vitality Room category, launched in 2017, is one of our most significant investments to date and takes our approach to Vitality to the next level. The Vitality Room began with understanding the needs and wants of our guests. We then applied our learnings and expertise in terms of innovative in-room technology and mindful, high-quality design. All to simplify, enhance and improve the guest experience – not to mention their quality of life when they stay with us. Innovation at Swissôtel should always benefit our people, planet and profit. The Vitality Rooms at our flagship property Swissôtel The Stamford in Singapore for instance demonstrates just that. The Vitality Rooms help guests to overcome jet lag through innovative light sources and ergonomic furniture and improve sleep quality through circadian lighting and natural materials.

Sustainable Excellence is in our DNA

As our business has grown in scale and complexity, we have continued to operate autonomously. We had to be resourceful and well-organized to run an efficient and effective hotel business. Very early on, it was clear that we needed to define and work to a clear operating purpose and approach. One that would preserve our Know-How, gain efficiency, help us to stay relevant and easily onboard new hotels that join the Swissôtel portfolio. Essential to our Sustainable Excellence approach is to look and learn outside as well as inside our industry. While not an easy balance, we find ways to harness creativity and innovation while still being bottom-line oriented. We continuously implement Sustainable Excellence initiatives to make sure our commitment to quality never fades. The proof is in the recognition awarded by the industry as well as our guests and colleagues. For a decade, Swissôtel has been the only global hotel company ISO certified in Quality Management, Environmental Management, Health and Safety Management and recognized for the European Excellence Award.

Teamwork: High-Quality Craftsmanship

At Swissôtel, we are all our craftswomen and craftsmen. We are professionals and pay attention to every detail in our daily work from striving to make the perfect bed and creating the perfect dish to selecting and pouring the perfect wine. We work together and take pride in shaping our distinct and unique guest experience that goes above and beyond what many consider to be hospitality. We craft an efficient and caring atmosphere infused with an intelligent, distinct, and high-quality design that's inspired by local customs around the world.

Making a mark in the world

Over the past decade, we invested in brand awareness studies on a global level and it is rewarding to see that Swissôtel consistently outperforms its footprint in terms of awareness. The brand is perceived as high-quality and is trending upwards in terms of well-being. Our strength as a brand lies in our Swiss origin and how we embody quality, efficiency and care. It is this positive brand image, especially in China and the USA, which offers the opportunity for us to price our product at a premium despite fierce competition. The fact that Swissôtel is even noticed in these key markets is remarkable, especially since the company operates only one hotel in the USA (Chicago) and four in China (Beijing, Shanghai, Foshan and Kunshan).

Our Claim is our Call to Action

Swiss at heart and global by nature, we believe in living life well and caring for the people and the world around us. It is our Swiss hospitality, synonymous with quality, efficiency and care that sets us apart and ensures our guests feel at ease and recharged. We summarize this in our brand claim introduced in 2017: 'Life is a journey. Live it well.' Many recent global studies indicate that more than two-thirds of the Millennials generation state that health is the most important thing in their lives. As these guests enter the workforce and start to travel for business as well as leisure, we want to continue to care for them as much as we care for our people.

Now part of Accor Group, the world's leading augmented hospitality group, Swissôtel has a strong base from which to grow and continue to succeed. Our Purpose of 'Bringing Quality in Life' is a broad canvas for us to shape the future; it is about enhancing the lives of everyone around us and accepting nothing less than the very best – then asking ourselves how we can do even better.

How momondo Opens Up The World

"A higher Purpose unites – and brings the world closer together."

Julie Pedersen
Contributing Author, Vice President
Communications at KAYAK

Case in Point: momondo's "Let's Open Our World"

For momondo, the story started in 2006: the online travel search engine was founded with a vision of opening the world and breaking down boundaries between countries, cultures and people. At its very heart, momondo was always about traveling with a Purpose; a Purpose to open the world.

A decade on, momondo has come a long way. The core product has grown into a set of innovative, inspirational travel services and features that are enabling people to explore new destinations and ways of travel. With this foundation established, for momondo the time was right to take the vision of an open world to the next level: a world without prejudice is a universally important and relevant cause to bring attention to. So, once and for all, we decided to infuse our vision into everything we did (which was not difficult, because it was so anchored in the identity of the brand) and start a conversation with travelers about the importance of breaking down boundaries between people through traveling.

Planning for Context

Researchers from Stanford University[167] have shown that friendships across cultures increase interest in learning more about others, and that cooperation between people with different backgrounds results in fewer prejudices about other cultural groups. Inspired by these studies, we set out to investigate the connection between travelling and open-mindedness. For our report *The Value of Traveling*, we surveyed 7200 people from 18 countries across North and South America, Europe, Africa, Asia and Australia. We found a statistically significant association between travel and trust in people of another nationality or religious beliefs. In short, we found that traveling makes us more trusting and open to the outside world. This transcends borders and underscores the importance of travelling to break down barriers.

However, discouraging as it may sound, we also saw signs of a world that is increasingly divided, and that current discourse tends more toward separation rather than unity. Forty-nine percent of the respondents in the report believe people are less tolerant toward other cultures today than five years ago. This finding made it very clear: there is a fight to be fought against growing intolerance, and momondo as a travel brand – particularly given our higher Purpose of opening the world – should play a role in bringing the world closer together.

Let's Open Our World

In 2016, momondo launched the "Let's Open Our World" platform. This is a Purpose platform for initiatives that give courage and encourage each one of us to stay curious and be open-minded so we can all enjoy a better, more diversified world. We partnered with CISV, a non-profit organization working to help the next generation be more open-minded by educating and inspiring action for peace. The Purpose of this organization is so closely aligned with momondo that we both recognized a partnership would not only strengthen our common Purpose and goals but allow us to work with future generations of travelers. Together we hosted a summer village in Brazil for 11-year-old's across a wide range of nationalities and later developed educational material for schools with a focus on tolerance and prejudice. Aside from the partnership with CISV, we also started a global foundation – the *Open World Projects* – to support innovative ideas that encourage diversity and open-mindedness.

Engaging and Activating Audiences Inside and Outside

To spark public conversation about the importance of breaking down boundaries between people through traveling, the marketing, product and communications teams at momondo joined forces to find ways to engage users. This has led to a number of initiatives – including the two lighthouse brand activations that I will highlight here – designed to encourage a global conversation on a topic that we believe is truly important.

The first activation was the DNA Journey (2016). The journey, documented on film, follows 67 individuals as they receive their ancestral DNA tests and realize that they are linked to the rest of the world, even parts of the world they may have felt prejudiced towards. The message at the core of the DNA Journey is that there are more things uniting us than dividing us. The campaign film has more than 600 million views online.

The second activation was The World Piece (2019); a visual, living manifestation of what it will take to bring the world closer together. We asked people from all over the world, each with a different story, to make a commitment – in the form of a single line tattoo on their back connecting them to 60 other individuals with a single line – to show that despite our differences, we are united in our humanity. And that the world can't fall apart if you dare to connect.

Activating on Purpose can generate massive attention and truly help increase global brand awareness. But success is hard to achieve without a rock-solid Purpose foundation to guide all efforts. By first establishing our vision and then building our Purpose platform, we have been able to develop communications with the knowledge that we are united behind a common goal that we all believe in, and which our audience can believe in too. This gives us the confidence to continue to create world-first, world-class Purpose communications.

On the Test of Time

"A nation may be said to consist of its territory, its people, and its laws. The territory is the only part which is of certain durability."

Abraham Lincoln
American Politician, Lawyer and President

The progressive pharaohs who led the great Egyptian civilization and built the ancient Egyptian pyramids have long passed away, yet ancient Egypt as a brand is immortal. Thousands of years later, architects, researchers, archaeologists, historians and scholars of today are still fascinated by Egyptian times. Timelessness means existing independent of time, outliving trend cycles and establishing a permanent status. Operating on Purpose and following *The Guiding Purpose Strategy* is essential to becoming timeless.

Visionaries and great leaders survive the test of time by staying in sync with their Purpose. If you are looking for a brief moment in the limelight, you are not a member of the Purpose club. *The Guiding Purpose Strategy* is the force behind the notion of heritage and legacy. Preserving heritage is part of the higher Purpose. People, companies, empires and civilizations come and go, but Purpose lives on to shape culture.

A timeless brand is one that has mastered the ability of not being tied to a particular phase in time. Such brands have managed to find the utmost profound Know-Why. Many luxury brands do this well. In fact, it is very difficult for a true luxury brand to die. Fabergé, the old Russian fine jewelry brand, was destroyed during its prime due to the Bolshevist Revolution. In 1917, the Bolsheviks brought a violent end to Faberge's ateliers, seizing their treasures, closing down production and forcing Fabergé and his family to flee. But Peter Carl Fabergé had already built a timeless brand, which is why after 90 years, the brand was able to revive itself and still persists today.

A. Lange & Söhne, a luxury watch brand, also survived political turmoil. The brand ceased to exist for the longest time until November 9, 1989. The collapse of the Iron Curtain gave Walter Lange the opportunity to bring his family's business back to life. While a strong brand may vanish from the market, it continues to exist in the collective consciousness of those who cherish it.

Brands have the ability to pass the test of time if they are led by a strong inner Purpose. In their prime, timeless brands touched the hearts and souls of their advocates – the very advocates who will always see to it that their most cherished brands carry on living.

Purpose Driving Organizational Culture

"Culture eats strategy for breakfast."

Prof. Peter F. Drucker
Austrian-born American Consultant and Author

According to a Deloitte Millennial Survey, Millennials overwhelmingly believe (75%) businesses are more focused on their own agendas than helping to improve society.[151] Younger generations will continue to look for meaning beyond profit and demand transparency in 'how we do business.' IBM, for example, uses social Purpose to attract top employees motivated to engage and boost overall performance. It is not about catering to their every whim; it is about helping them make their best contribution to your organization. It's about meeting the challenges and expectations of the Gen Y workforce.

Today's young people are not just younger versions of you – they have different expectations of life and work, and they're shaking things up to induce change. Studies have shown that meaning is so important to people that they actively go about re-crafting their jobs to enhance their sense of meaningfulness.[152] A new generation of talent has the potential to add energy, innovation and freshness to your organization. But at the same time, they can be disruptive, challenging and energy-sapping. In their book called *Real Luxury*, Misha Pinkhasov and Rachna Joshi Nair describe how Generation X and Y view professional life:

> *Generation X and Y (...) no longer feel obliged to aim for the security that a corporate career path provides. To these generations, work looks more like a productive form of play rather than toil. If the baby boomers are thinking about work-life balance, the younger generations are focused on work-life blending where both form a single, pleasurable existence.*[153]

During a Q&A session at Yale University, Eric Schmidt, former CEO of Google, said: "One of the things you learn about decision-making is that you don't want a single person making the decision, you want groups making decisions and you want those groups to be making decisions under the principle of 'we will make the best decision not the consensus decision.' [...] We [at Google] will sit there and debate until everyone says that's the best idea as opposed to warring consensus arguments." Fostering an open dialogue that encourages inclusive decisions requires more than an open attitude and a mindset that can think beyond ego. It requires a carefully crafted mix of people, behavior and vision. The prefix to operating in such a mode is a culture of excellence based on values and ambition – which in turn is, of course, intrinsically linked to the very reason why we exist.

How should a leader who is trying to create a strong culture within the organization look at this concept? Organizational culture can only be cultivated and maintained if all acknowledge the fact that the best result would come from everyone in the group doing what is best for himself or herself and the group. So, then, what is the most optimal way of achieving this as a leader? The answer is hidden in plain sight: by making the transition to become Purpose-led. Research by IMD and Burson Marsteller "provides strong evidence that leadership is a strong and consistent predictor of authentic corporate Purpose, explaining almost 50% of the variance in perceptions of authenticity."[154]

Becoming a Purpose-led brand and organization is not a mathematical issue – it's a geometrical one. Euclid, often referred to as the 'Father of Geometry,' was an ancient Greek intellectual who created an axiomatic system worth remembering. Euclid stated that if two things are equal to the same thing, they are equal to each other. If all the individuals within a company (including the leadership) can be equal to the brand rather than the leader or the CEO, they would all be equal to each other. A strong set of arguments can't unite people, but a strong philosophy can. A mathematical model may be able to connect individuals, but a geometrical model can unify them. In other words, a successful company can't do what a successful brand can, namely bond teams together. It represents a uniting canvas for shared and aligned Purpose.

Leonid Matsih, philosopher and theologian, stated in one of his lectures that rituals help us sense the meaning of life. Activities with ritualistic value include drawing, meditating, dancing, creative writing, playing a musical instrument and singing. We are not suggesting that you implement a Walmart- style 'morning chant' with your staff to kick off your daily business routine. But if you are Price Waterhouse Coopers and your Purpose is '*To build trust in society and solve important problems*,'[155] then creating a trustworthy working environment is key. Subtle, institutionalized rituals such as five-minute insight-sharing sessions every morning for instance can help create an environment of stimulation.

For the culture to thrive rather than merely survive Purpose alone is not enough. There needs to be a durable formula for the workforce's fulfillment. Dr Ernest Dichter found in his research that "the 'why' and the 'how to' of human motivations are interrelated." Which is why this formula needs to be based on not only on the 'why' but also on the 'how.' As Tony Schwartz and Christine Porath summarized the *how* of work in their article 'Why You Hate Work':

> *The way we are working isn't working. (…) For most of us,*
> *in short, work is a depleting, dispiriting experience, and in*
> *some obvious ways, it's getting worse. (…) Demand for our*
> *time is increasingly exceeding our capacity — draining us of*
> *the energy we need to bring our skill and talent fully to life.*
> *Increased competitiveness and a leaner, post-recession work*
> *force add to the pressures. The rise of digital technology is*

perhaps the biggest influence, exposing us to an unprecedented flood of information and requests that we feel compelled to read and respond to at all hours of the day and night.[156]

The source of many major issues in the day-to-day business life most likely derive from the fact that a large proportion of businesspeople are going through their work hours by applying a series of insignificant little Know-Hows while the other minority of them are advocating the Know-Whys. What is being overlooked is that the Know-How needs to be complemented (not separated) with the Know-Why. Everything has been figured out except how to work.[157] Is it not strange that we have simplified almost every business process, accelerated the speed of every communication tool, brought all apps in one mobile phone, got access to unprecedented amounts of information etc. and yet we are still left with the need of extending our work hours, feeling more stressed, experiencing pressure and burnouts? When the Know-How and the Know-Why are together instead of replacing each other, we could work smarter instead of just harder. Working hard is a culture of devotion. Working right is a culture of excellence.

Shared and aligned Purpose is a must-have to build strong cultures. It provides employees with a sense of belonging and helps them understand their role within the bigger picture. Research conducted by McKinsey confirms that meaning drives higher workplace productivity and in turn growth and profit.[158] So how then does Purpose propel growth?

How Purpose Propels Growth

"Without continual growth and progress, such words as improvement, achievement, and success have no meaning."

Benjamin Franklin
Polymath, Diplomat and one of the
Founding Fathers of the US

Liam Byrne identified shared characteristics of the giant entrepreneurs-magnates that built Britain during the First Industrial Revolution and concluded that "the very best of entrepreneurs have higher-level objectives. This sense of purpose guides many of the Leap 100 entrepreneurs, and they, like all of us, should be inspired by our incredible ancestors."[159] Fast forward to today, shares of meaningful companies have gone up approximately 600% on a 10-year average.[160] There is a growing tendency of both large and small organizations to prioritize the inner Know-Why to navigate in the new economic environment of the 21st century. More and more large companies are joining the Purpose-led revolution.

The Ernst & Young Beacon Institute, which was launched at the 2015 World Economic Forum in Davos, joined forces with the Saïd Business School at the University of Oxford and Harvard Business Review Analytic Services to begin transforming businesses through the principle of Purpose. According to their research, 87% of 474 global executives believe companies perform best in the long-term if their Purpose goes beyond the bottom line of financial results.[161] All challenges related to trust, leadership, employee engagement, efficiency, branding, sustainability, entrepreneurship and innovation are being reoriented with one powerful component that can hold the entire temple of commerce together – Purpose.

One of the most common mistakes companies make is to confuse Purpose with corporate social responsibility (CSR). Yes, every properly Purpose-driven enterprise is sustainable, ethical and socially responsible. However, not every business with a CSR section in its annual report is a meaningful, Purpose-led business. In 1987, the *Brundtland Report* defined sustainability in business as "development that meets the needs of the present without compromising the ability of future generations to meet their own needs."[162]

Sustainability, laterally speaking, is divided into three branches – environmental, social and economic. The environmental side is obviously about the ecological health of our planet, the social side is about the overall wellbeing of employees within a company and its supply chains and, finally, the economic side is about generating enough money to pay for the former and some. What is interesting is that whilst there is quite a lot of media coverage about the first two elements, there is very little on the economic impact. We believe that without a strong inner Purpose at work, increasing revenue and profit will be harder to achieve in the future. Indeed, Purpose and profits are increasingly intertwined.

In order to fully comprehend the blend of making profits and helping society, it is useful to look at it from a personal perspective. If you, as an individual, are trying to achieve self- actualization by working on yourself for yourself, you are least likely to achieve it since it is a rather an egotistical aim. However, if you are trying to develop yourself to be a better husband or a better corporate partner, it is a different story. This means you are improving for yourself and for others. This approach doesn't just emphasize the idea of serving. Rather, it provides the model whereby transforming and improving yourself first will allow you to give back. So, in other words, Purpose is just as much about the impact on the lives of the founder, chairman, the board of directors, and employees as it is about the impact on customers, linking back to our concept of shared and aligned Purpose.

The idea of shared and aligned Purpose should never be perceived as an image of soldiers standing in artificially symmetrical order. It is to be pictured as the natural order of the red seeds inside a pomegranate. The positioning of each seed is aesthetically unique, fine-tuned, and organic. Purpose is the source of energy that sets things in motion. It drives the organization or the individual to prosperity with its force of motivation and aspiration. Employees of Purpose-driven organizations go the extra mile because it is motivating to be able contribute to meaning beyond their paycheck.

Think of the new educational tech company Coursera. It doesn't merely promise to democratize education; it actually delivers it. Coursera makes courses from the most prestigious universities around the world accessible no matter where you reside. The Purpose is genuine and hidden within the company's mission statement of 'Providing universal access to the world's best education.' It is not quite as aptly worded as we would want it to be, but it is meaningful in that it directly addresses the global challenges of education. As UNESCO reports, the number of out-of-school children is on the rise from 124 million.[163] Coursera's overarching Purpose transcends money and gives the brand a meaning with which employees, students and stakeholders alike can whole-heartedly identify.

Purpose is not only a key corporate economic booster. It is also important on an individual level. One of the greatest aspects of Purpose is its capacity to advance intuition by encouraging clear introspection. A problem among professionals, entrepreneurs and leaders is that they perceive Purpose as something extrinsic. This train of thought leads to the failure of aligning intention with action. Taking the next step is pointless when your intentions are not clear. Purpose is often conflated with aims, goals, objectives, etc. However, a *Guiding Purpose Strategy* is of absolute intrinsic value. It is the discovery of the Know-Why.

Making it Happen

Conquering Time

"Everything has been figured out, except how to live."

Jean-Paul Sartre
French Existentialist

We live in times of acceleration. Technology moves faster than most of us can grasp and constant change is the new norm. Yet, since the very beginning of recorded history the notion of time has always been the one thing in this world that no one can fully conquer. Nobody has been able to capture 25 hours in a day or nine days in a week. However, it doesn't take being a great analyst to see that some perceive and use their time significantly better than others.

Why do some of the busiest people seem to use time significantly better than others? Purpose-driven professionals, entrepreneurs and leaders use their time better because they adopt a certain way of thinking in regards to the notion of time. As Leonardo da Vinci once stated: "Time stays long enough for anyone who will use it." Having this mindset means, first of all, respecting and valuing one's own time. Embedding a Purpose-driven strategy is not a quick win – it will take time.

People have the habit of asking "How much time do I have?" But maybe this is not the right question to ask to start with. Perhaps, asking the opposite would be more appropriate: "How much of me does time have?" – time can consume us if we do not know how to master it.

Here is a familiar example: you go to your inbox to see if you have received the email you have been waiting for. Even though this can be done in a matter of seconds, you get distracted and end up watching a 12-minute 'short' video, all whilst a friend pings over a nice but unimportant WhatsApp message – and you decide to take a look and reply. Before you know it, 30 minutes have passed instead of the 30 seconds it should have taken to check on that email. Procrastination works in similar ways, picking the easy things first, delaying the important stuff until we eventually have no other option than to tackle it.

The reason behind such time-wasting behavior is strongly linked to attention and time. A recent study by Microsoft found that a digital lifestyle has made it more difficult for us to stay focused, with the human attention span shortening from 12 seconds to eight seconds in less than a decade.[164] Being focused and determined on one or several prespecified things is the way to avoid distraction and wasting time.

Time is perceived in different ways in different cultures, but all agree on one thing: time changes everything and the only thing that doesn't change is change itself.

There are two fundamental ways of looking at how time is spent:

1. As time passes, value is lost

2. As time passes, value increases

Some people grow weaker and more passive as they get older, while others get wiser and more important with age. What about brands? Michael Eisner, former CEO of The Walt Disney Company, offers the perfect answer: "A brand is a living entity – and it is enriched or undermined cumulatively over time, the product of a thousand small gestures."

While many business leaders say one should spend *more* time on self-development, Peter Drucker, the legendary management consultant and author, used to say you should "organize your self-development." The two approaches are very different. Organizing does not mean doing more of the same thing but structuring it in an optimum way. What is the simplest way of structuring and organizing self-development? And how can we use it to help us activate the power of Purpose?

To conquer time, three important angles have to complement each other: *MeTime, SocialTime and ProductiveTime*. The latter is directly linked to 'what we do' and 'how to do it.' It seems only logical then to spend enough time thinking about 'why we do what we do' before focusing on making the most out of it.

The Triangle of Time

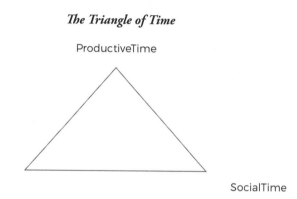

ProductiveTime

MeTime   SocialTime

MeTime

There is a series of things that we do during the week which are so basic that we hardly think about them. But what if we redefined activities such as walking the dog or watering the plants as *MeTime*? We would then perceive these activities as stimulating tasks to foster contemplation, instead of mere banal responsibilities. Making the most of *MeTime* requires a conscious reflection on what to do with the time for oneself. Here are a few tips to get started:

Designate a portion of the day to contemplate and plan

This is taking the time to contemplate specific aspects of your life that require finding solutions, analyzing for the short- or mid-term, thinking about goals, making a Plan B, etc.

Designate a portion of the day to dream
This is when the doors of perception are wide open and you allow your limitless imagination to float freely; thinking is as broad as vast oceans, the tallest mountains and widest deserts, a moment of reflection in which everything becomes possible.

Designate a portion of the day to meditate
There is a certain state of being, a level above all levels that words cannot reach nor teach. Or in timeless words of Rumi, the 13th-century Sufi philosopher and jurist: "Out beyond ideas of wrongdoing and right doing, there is a field. I'll meet you there. When the soul lies down in that grass, the world is too full to talk about."

Me Time also includes spending time on social or cultural entertainment, leisure activities and hobbies, whether they are done collectively or individually. The way you structure your time with such activities is crucial. Throughout history, humanity has witnessed countless discoveries and inventions that changed the course of history. More often than not such monumental ideas were born during the trivialities of *Me Time* – taking a shower, playing a violin, daydreaming, etc.

During his speech at the Stanford Graduate School of Business, Sir James Wolfensohn, the ninth President of the World Bank, spoke of spending one's time:

> *If there is one thing that I would as a generality say to you, it is that if it is possible for you, in whatever you are doing to engage yourself in things other than the straight business course, you will find that not only does it enrich your life, but the truth of the matter is that it'll enrich your business.* [165]

Spending time is perceived as an investment. The link between attention and time is always something to keep in mind. Those that don't value this notion run the risk of not being able to grasp the intricacies of governing time.

SocialTime

SocialTime is not (only) about being on Snapchat or Facebook. By *SocialTime* we mean spending time with friends, family or colleagues at the coffee machine at work. It refers to the time spent not directly producing or solving work problems. Often a static picture of the traditional family is what commonly comes to mind when we think about *SocialTime*. However, we need to be careful about what we mean by this. According to Gillian Hampsen-Thompson, Professor of Education at the University of Sussex, "The 'traditional family' is something of a post-war invention – and the idealism that surrounds it is seriously flawed. Families are complex and fluid units."[166] One needs to acknowledge the fact that a family is not a static institution and that trying to uphold the engineered image of a perfect family is consuming. The same goes for friends. The goal is to find an environment where we can detach from routine and enjoy the richness of unconstrained emotions, lean on a friend's shoulder and most importantly, learn and grow. It is being able to know where family, friends and social activities fit in terms of our inner value system, so we can get the most out of *SocialTime*.

If we manage to balance *MeTime, SocialTime and ProductiveTime* we move ourselves into the pole position to successfully align with our inner Purpose. Without a doubt, *ProductiveTime* is where most issues arise; either because we don't have enough time to do it all or simply because we are not good enough at how we do what we do. Since we spend most of our working lives 'doing' or what we call *ProductiveTime,* this dominant area also affects our *MeTime* and *SocialTime.*

The following chapter lists a collection of tried and tested techniques to help master the domain of *ProductiveTime.*[167]

Entrepreneurial Focus

"Don't try to run before you walk – dig deep and take the time to think, it pays back in multiples."

Byron Smith
Contributing Author, CEO of XSpace and Serial Entrepreneur

Perhaps the most important thing to do before embarking on your new venture is understanding yourself. What are you really trying to achieve? Not spending enough time to cracking your inner way of organizing will hurt you further down the lane. It is not easy however, because the entrepreneurial drive – especially in today's fast paced environment – often leads to action before thought. With our most recent venture XSpace, we dedicated the time to think and dig deep, uncovering the needs of our tarot audience and getting into their hearts and minds before we even conceptualized the value proposition. It is magical to uncover the reason why you do what you do before you get going – and it helps guide all activities, providing focus for everyone involved. For XSpace, we uncovered that we weren't in the business of selling blank commercial condominium space, but in fact enabling freedom!

In my professional endeavors, I have come across way too many people who start companies by rattling off product or project features hoping that something might stick – spark interest and result in someone paying for it.

It is the opposite of articulating first what you are trying to achieve, what your company is about. This lack of Purpose translates into offerings that don't resonate with the customers and, as we've experienced firsthand, doesn't inspire any world-class thinking to help you build your company.

Through my personal experience of successes and failures in the start-up space, I can reflect on what works and what doesn't. A large part of failure can be linked to trying to be everything to everyone – which is a great way to slowly bleed a young company to death. The successes have a common theme too. In companies that fly, time is spent on reflection. Going deep, taking the plunge and workshop your way through competition, audiences and possibilities all the way through positioning and translating all of this into a cohesive communications strategy is key. A strong Purpose secretly flies under the radar and helps guide almost every facet of the business; from making the sales process more efficient, to the design colors on a wall, the way we build our products all the way to the people we don't want to target i.e.; the people we deliberately say 'no' to.

A sound sense of Purpose allows new entrepreneurs to know when to say 'no' in a survivalist environment – it is a hard thing to do. Again, through experience, I can comfortably say that understanding your Purpose has given me the confidence to say no and remain focused. I would highly recommend allocating some time and capital to any start-up to get the Purpose equation right at the start.

The best way to remedy a lot of the above rocky road scenarios to success is to take a deep breath before you start. At a more practical level, a guiding Purpose saves you time, which is the most precious commodity of newly forming companies, and this allows you to remain laser focused on creating great customer experiences and a really valuable company.

Productivity Mantra

"We are what we repeatedly do.
Excellence, then, is not an act, but a habit."

Aristotle
Greek Polymath

Stop multitasking

Computers are made for multitasking. Humans operate better when focusing on one task at a time. We can derive a great deal of power from developing a laser focus on a particular task at hand. Doing one thing at a time, doing it well and doing it right the first time.

Eliminate distractions

Convenience is the mother of distraction, so make it difficult to satisfy temptations. Shut down desktop notifications, your email program, the browser, leave your phone behind, close the door or move to a different room to get stuff done.

Show focus

Signal to others that you are not to be disturbed. If you work in an open space, put a sign on top of your screen that reads 'FOCUS.'

Focus your meetings

People generally don't need as much time as they request – give them half of the time they ask for. This forces everyone to be brief, clear and to the point. This is efficiency, without being unkind.

Create productivity rituals

Prioritize one key task to accomplish per day. Checking emails in the afternoon helps you reserve the peak energy hours of your mornings for your best work. Work in 90-minute intervals with short breaks. Structure your day and follow a rhythm.

Write a Stop-Doing list

Every productive person obsessively sets To-Do lists. But the experts also record what they consciously commit not to do.

Get up earlier

Use your morning to seize the day: mind over mattress. Get up an hour earlier.

Exercise

Exercise is energizing and makes us healthier. Additionally, exercise can improve our mood for up to 12 hours after we work out. Work out for at least 20 minutes a day. Feel better. Be smarter. Be less stressed. Have a more productive day.

Use your mind for thinking, not remembering

The best way to have a good idea is to have a lot of ideas. Note them down when they are fresh and use active thinking time later to develop or discard them. Thinking time shouldn't be something to get around to when you get a chance. Schedule two hours of *Me Time* each Tuesday morning.

Make technology your friend

There's a wealth of programs to help increase productivity: Evernote to keep track of tasks, lists and things to read-later, Dropbox to store files, WebEx to host webinars, Hootsuite to schedule social media posts and so on.

Just say no

Protect your time – the one asset no one can afford to waste. Say 'no' at least as often as you say yes. You can be polite while protecting time. And remember, scarcity yields desirability.

Get enough sleep

Most of us constantly have our fingers on the fast-forward button, when we really need to hit pause for a while. You can only carry on not sleeping enough for a while before it catches up with you.

Automate

Write down your daily routine, from getting up, to exercising, to what to wear and eat, to when you go to bed. Then follow through. No rule without exceptions, but structure helps us focus our energy on the important things. Productivity is not about luck. It is about commitment.

Use the commute

If you commute for 30 minutes each way everyday use that time to listen to great audiobooks or catch up on social media when in a train.

Live in the now

Practice active listening, pay attention and remain focused when interacting with people at work and at home. Note that attention is reciprocal – you get back what you give.

Disconnect

Don't be so available to everyone. Stop the 24/7 connectivity urge. Turn off your devices and think, create, plan and write. Zero interruptions. Pure focus. Great results.

Branding Thyself

"Be yourself, everyone else is already taken."

Oscar Wilde
Irish poet and playwright

Some call it self-marketing, others call it personal branding. The notion of branding ourselves is largely misunderstood. We must first avoid the confusing terms of self-marketing or personal branding. A more useful term is perhaps 'branding thyself.' Notice that we intentionally change it from *self* to *thyself* in order to emphasize that this is based on your world within. Why is branding thyself becoming ever more crucial and what are the intricate nuances of branding thyself?

In times of increased transparency and exposure, the idea of creating one's own brand to underpin a particular value proposition, an area of expertise and so on is no longer an act of magic. Applying the same tested and tried frameworks that help corporates define, refine, position and communicate their brands successfully is available to any individual aiming to propel his or her own brand into the future. The frameworks outlined in the previous chapter The GPS Framework works just as well for individuals.

However, putting up a profile on LinkedIn and writing a few blog posts is not enough. Making it all look nice is not that complex. Sticking it on a good website with good visual differentiation is a bit trickier, but still nothing out of the ordinary. For most people, the biggest struggle is to be clear about who they really are, not who they want to be.

When we analyze the creation of effective value systems that lead to outstanding examples of branding thyself, we find that in this context 'the origin' is the message. On an individual 'branding' level, Purpose is the message. Since each of us on this planet has something unique within, the number of 'personal brands' that can potentially be built is astronomical.

It is possible to develop a personal philosophy and become the great architect of your innate universe with the aim to create an infinite *Youniverse*. Remember that people are no longer going to be satisfied with your outer appearance. Appearance is not out of the equation, but it definitely is no longer enough for *branding thyself*. The more meaningful your cosmos within, the more essential your essence is to the audience. Generation Y and beyond wants to see your Know-Why. Getting your makeup done professionally, and sharing cute photos on social media is not enough. It lacks Purpose. You must also be photogenic from within. Think of the many examples of the luxury brands we cited in this book. Many share key elements of their internal cultures, their higher Purpose and some of their secret Know-How. Turning oneself inside out is about revealing what really goes on behind the scenes and why. The inner cult that is derived from your inner Purpose manifests a culture to the outer world, which can be brought to life through the discipline of brand management. Creating a profile, a website, a video and so on is only going to be consistent and integral if it reflects your inner self.

Saying something in an *outrospe*ctive way rather than in an introspective way can be perceived as copying or paraphrasing. In other words, target audiences wouldn't perceive it as sincere or original. What can be accepted as genuinely new and legitimate is the message that comes from the inner-why. For example, take Sir Richard Branson, founder of the Virgin Group. He is incredibly good at branding himself. Why? Because he has absolute clarity on his Purpose in life. Sir Richard Branson is a visionary who has a set of values that is vividly embedded within his brand. He became a business magnate because he always stayed true to his higher Purpose within of 'Changing business for good' and he never hesitates to project it onto the outer world. It is worth visiting Virgin's website to appreciate how deeply Richard Branson believes in the power of Purpose.[168]

Elon Musk, CEO and product architect of Tesla Motors is also one of the entrepreneurs who has mastered the mechanics of branding thyself rather than merely dwelling in lavish self- promotion. He runs Tesla Inc., SpaceX, SolarCity – all at once. It is not incidental that Elon Musk devotes so much of his time brand managing his internal self. As a serial entrepreneur, the time invested in branding the world within is not time lost but time spent intelligently.

The complexity of choice and the growing number of communication channels underlines how branding thyself will function as an enabler to unleash the power of personal Purpose in the years ahead. We believe that self-branding will form part of the core skills people need to develop in the next 25 years. In a world where the consumer[169] has the power, having the ability to market oneself is key. Tom Peter notes: "All of us need to understand the importance of branding. We are CEOs of our own companies: Me Inc. To be in business today, our most important job is to be head marketer for the brand called You."[170] Let not your short-term interests, but your innate Purpose be your guiding principle.

Cultivating the Culture of the Self

*"It is in constantly paying attention to oneself
that one assures one's salvation."*

Gaius Musonius Rufus
Roman Stoic Philosopher

People, countries, industries and (some) brands have culture. However, culture does not have to be a collective phenomenon only. Some individuals do have a private inner culture within, which they build throughout their lifetime. In ancient times, the Greek and Roman philosophers called it 'the culture of the self.' Unlike animals, human beings are conscious, thinking beings. Therefore, the need for cultivating a culture of the self is a natural need. Yet, few succeed at it. Epictetus, the ancient Stoic philosopher, once said: "Men are this unique kind of beings on earth who have to take care of themselves. Nature has provided animals with everything they need, humans don't have the same natural equipment, but we must understand that the necessity of taking care of ourselves is also a supplementary gift, which has been bestowed." So, what is the benefit of creating an individual culture? Why do decision-makers, managers, marketers or anyone trying to master any craft need to keep developing and cultivating this culture of the self?

Inner culture provides a larger space for the times when the outside world seems too limiting. Inner culture offers us a kind of inner dynamo that contributes to personal skills such as intuition, introspection, imagination, etc. It is about having the ability to create your own legend about life itself. It is not a list of values about virtue, ethics and righteousness – these are too abstract to be intuitive. Rather, this is about constructing a system of values. The culture of the self is a great meaning system that helps maintain the *multiple personality order*. But, above all, it is about having a Purpose in one's life, providing guidance during the stormy adventures throughout life's journey.

Developing a culture of the self requires one to be concerned with oneself for the sake of others AND to be concerned with oneself for oneself. Caring for oneself is not a new concept. Greek and Roman philosophers called it *epimeleia heautou* (Greek for 'care of self') and it was one of the main principles of ethics and a key rule in the art of living for an entire millennium. One should take into account that it is never too early and never too late to occupy oneself with one's true essence, with one's true self. Gaius Musonius Rufus, a Roman Stoic philosopher of the 1st century stated: "It is in the act of constantly paying attention to oneself that one assures one's salvation."

The 20th-century French philosopher and philologist Michel Foucault gave a triumphant lecture at UC Berkeley on the culture of the self in 1983. During this lecture he said: "What was the most important moral principle, the most characteristic in ancient philosophy? The answer, which comes immediately to mind, is not *epimeleia heautou* ('care of the self') but, as you know, *gnōthi seauton*, which is, know thyself." Perhaps the Western historical and philosophical tradition has somehow overrated the importance of the 'know yourself.' In the Far East there are teachings that explain how being too aware of yourself doesn't help in taking care of yourself. Cultivating the culture of the self requires conscious self-mastery.

We believe that understanding and consciously applying a *Guiding Purpose Strategy* is most essential. The existential Know-Why is already becoming the new operational Know-How. Our children and grandchildren will advance *The Guiding Purpose Strategy* even further. Cultivating the self will be integrated into our lifestyles to the extent that *The Guiding Purpose Strategy* will encompass one's private, social and business life.

As Buckminster Fuller would agree, the children of the future will do what needs to be done, as they will be aware of the fact that that is how the universe designed itself. We firmly believe that people will increasingly use tools such as applying a *Guiding Purpose Strategy* to change the world for the better. The leaders of the future will use their inner Know-Why to adapt the world to them rather than adapting themselves to a limited pre-defined worldview.

True Purpose that radiates from within cannot be separated from personal mastery of the inner self. As brand makers, business builders and individuals, the only way forward is not just to pass on what we have built. We must take advantage of our ability and Know-How to advance the Know-Why for generations to come.

The Last Word

Wanderer Above the Mist
Caspar David Friedrich, 1818

Like a child's first visit to a dazzling circus
An exciting feeling you cannot purchase
Discovering this deep inner Purpose
Oh, being aware of its guiding service

To articulate it and bring it to surface
To record it poetically in endless verses
To the point when we are left wordless
To, finally, escape all cycles and circuits

One inner cult of yours,
From which all culture will derive
A vast blue ocean of fortune
Patiently waiting for you to dive
Hidden within, as an intuitive drive
An inner voice of growth, of being alive
To navigate upwards, not to merely survive
Transcending cycles, to finally thrive!

By Tofig Husein-zadeh

We cannot but hope that the consolidated words, expertise, frameworks and wisdom of great minds both past and present have achieved at least one thing: to help you, the reader to advance your thinking, to stimulate your mind, your understanding and your ambition to use the power of Purpose to bring about positive change.

It is our deepest hope that consciously embedding Purpose from within will yield positive growth. For leaders, brands, organizations and their cultures – and to everyone on this planet more generally.

Onwards and Upwards!

Index

Contributing Authors

Dr Sionade Robinson

Associate Dean, People & Culture,
Cass Business School, London

Leading a highly ranked MBA and many Executive Education programs at a global leading business school, as well as ten years of running my own consulting firm, taught me a lot about identifying talented leaders who conceive and deliver new value and game changing results.

What began as a professional interest in how an Explorer's Mindset can add value for global employers has now become a personal obsession, from analyzing the lessons of incredible dramas of famous expeditions, gathering insights from leading explorers in many fields, to how NASA is using the history of exploration to select the best crews for Mars, applying an Explorer's Mindset is a new frontier of leadership development for organizations.

Dr Graeme Codrington

Futurist, speaker, author and CEO of strategy firm, TomorrowToday Global.

Graeme Codrington is an expert on the future of work. He is a researcher, author, futurist, presenter and board advisor working across multiple industries and sectors. He has a particular interest in disruptive forces changing how people live, work, interact and connect with each other. Speaking internationally to over 100,000 people in more than 20 different countries every year, his client list includes some of the world's top companies, and CEOs invite him back time after time to share his latest insights and help them and their teams gain a clear understanding of how to successfully prepare for the future.

Graeme is the co-founder and international director of TomorrowToday, a global firm of futurists and business strategists.

Willi Helbling

Chief Executive Officer,
Business Professionals Network

Willi Helbling completed a Business Management education at the University of St. Gallen and is Chief Executive Officer of the BPN Foundation (www.bpn.ch). The BPN Foundation promotes entrepreneurs in developing and emerging countries. The philosophy behind BPN Foundation is to assist and guide entrepreneurs to eventually be self-sufficient. Before assuming management responsibilities at BPN, he worked as an independent Management Consultant for more than two decades.

Helbling is married and the father of two adult daughters, working in medicine and marketing. He lives outside of Zurich and – as long as his commitments will allow – he relaxes by playing golf and by spending time in the Engadine mountains.

Dr Dimitrios Tsivrikos

University College London
Consumer and Business Psychologist

Dr Dimitrios Tsivrikos is a Consumer and Business Psychologist at University College London (UCL). His research, teaching and consultancy work specialize in Business, Consumer/Branding and Occupational Psychology with a specialist interest in the contribution of social identity and group membership to a range of organizational processes, such as leadership, communication, organizational change, advertising, and Mergers and Acquisitions (M&A).

He has held a number of international research fellowships, and has published widely on psychology and business-oriented subjects. He is a leading commentator on consumer behavior and a frequent guest on the BBC, as well as acted as a scientific consultant in various periodicals such as *Sunday Times*, *Esquire* and the *Guardian*.

Jean-Francois Hirschel

Founder of H-Ideas

Reto Zangerl

Founder of Brand Affairs

Jean-François Hirschel is the founder and CEO of H-IDEAS, a company which aims at re-establishing trust in the financial world. His professional expertise lies in strategically positioning financial services companies at brand and product level.

Jean-François has held senior leadership positions at Paribas, Société Générale and Unigestion. He holds a MSc from EPFL Lausanne, Switzerland, and has profound knowledge and experience in Institutional, Private and Retail Banking & Asset Management.

Reto Zangerl studied business administration at the University of St Gallen (M.A. HSG). He founded Brand Affairs in 2006, specializing in brand strategy, public relations, and social media, employing 26 consultants and counselors in Switzerland, Germany and Austria.

His references involve iconic brands such as Harley-Davidson, Chiquita or Miele and he acted as speaker for Starbucks Coffee Switzerland during more than ten years. Before starting his own business, he worked as brand manager at Unilever and as consultant at Atkinson Stuart and Bütikofer & Company. Reto is board member of the Swiss healthy food restaurant brand "not guilty" and currently lives, near Zurich, Switzerland.

Lilian Roten

Vice President Brand Management
Swissôtel Hotels & Resorts and
Pullman Hotels

Lilian has over 25 years of experience in the tourism and hospitality industry. A principal architect of the Swissôtel brand and responsible for returning the Pullman brand to its growth track, Lilian continues to lead their successful evolution. She oversees the brand strategy teams in Zurich and Paris to ensure brand integrity through a consistent brand experience in products and services, ambiance and design, culture and behavior, and marketing and communications.

Lilian is a graduate of École Hôtelière de Lausanne and holds a Post Graduate Diploma in Innovation & Strategy from Oxford University and an Advanced Certificate in Luxury from HEC Paris.

Julie Pedersen

Vice President Communications at
KAYAK

Julie is an award-winning brand communications expert with 10+ years of international communications experience. As Vice President of Communications, she oversees communications in the EMEA region across six different brands, including KAYAK, momondo, Cheapflights, SWOODOO and Checkfelix, as well as the world's largest restaurant booking platform, OpenTable.

Julie was acknowledged in "The Innovator 25 – EMEA" in 2017 by Holmes Report, listing individuals who are reshaping the marketing and communications world. Julie holds an MA in International Business Communications from Copenhagen Business School.

Byron Smith
CEO of XSpace and Serial Entrepreneur

Ivan Schouker
Managing Partner and Founder at Finarchitects

Byron is a Sydney-born entrepreneur based in New York with a family business background in commercial property – his most recent venture is XSpace in which he is co-founder and investor. He's also active in the automotive-technology industry as co-founder of artificial intelligence company Ai Automotive Inc and advanced materials company P1 Graphene Solutions Ltd.

Across Australia, UK and USA, Byron has successfully led multimillion-dollar fund raises, created and executed marketing strategies, built financial structures and spearheaded business development for the ventures he's involved with.

Byron received his Bachelor of Commerce from Macquarie University, Sydney and his MBA from Cass Business School, London. He currently resides in New York City with his wife Anna and regularly spends time in Sydney and Texas for family and work.

Ivan Schouker is Managing Partner at Finarchitects, an advisory and venture firm accompanying investors, entrepreneurs and management teams. His engagements focus on technology, finance, professional services organizations and foundations as chief executive, board member, operating partner or adviser.

He previously led transformations as chief executive of two international banking businesses at American Express, then Toronto Dominion, at an Asian family-owned financial services group, as well as a principal at Booz Allen & Hamilton (now PWC Strategy&) in Hong Kong, London, New York and Washington D.C.

Ivan began his career in investment banking at Banque Paribas (now BNP Paribas) in New York and Taiwan. He holds degrees from Columbia University, the London School of Economics, and the Institut d'Etudes Politiques de Paris. He lectures on change management at the Geneva School of Economics and Management (University of Geneva) and was a co-author of "*Outsourcing and Human Resource Management*" (Routledge, 2007).

Notes

Endnotes

Initiation

1 Smith, Shaun. "Customer Experience: On Purpose." Brand Quarterly. 30 Sept. 2016. <http://www.brandquarterly.com/customer-experience-on-Purpose.>

2 Job Satisfaction Index 2015. Happiness Research Institute. Krifa. TNS Gallup

3 Lepitak, Stephen. "Don't Start a Business, Build a Brand: Sir John Hegarty on Working in the Startup Sector." The Drum. 02 May 2017. <http://www.thedrum.com/news/2017/05/02/ dont-start-business-build-brand-sir-john-hegarty-working-the-startup-sector>.

4 https://www.interbrand.com/best-brands/best-global-brands/2019/ranking/apple/ accessed 26 November 2019

5 Meaningful Brands Powered by Havas. N.p., n.d. Web. <http://www.meaningful-brands.com/en>.

6 "Cartography." Merriam-Webster, <http://www.merriam-ebster.com/dictionary/cartography>.

7 McLuhan, Marshall. Understanding Media. London: Sphere, 1973

8 Watson, James D. and Norton Zinder. "Genome Project Maps Paths of Diseases and Drugs." New York Times. 12 Oct. 1990. <http://www.nytimes. com/1990/10/13/opinion/l-genome-project-maps-paths-of-diseases-and-drugs-239090. html>

9 ibid

10 Trevor, Jonathan. "News." Saïd Business School. University of Oxford, 20 May 2016. <http:// www.sbs.ox.ac.uk/school/news/best-companies-are-best-aligned?utm_source=Twitter&utm_medium=link&utm_campaign=Corporate_JonathanTrevorHandles_JUN16>.

11 Note: The term and concept were coined in 1987 by Frank White who explored the theme in his book The Overview Effect – Space Exploration and Human Evolution (Houghton-Mifflin, 1987), (AIAA, 1998)

12 Harvard Business Review, Working Knowledge <https://hbswk.hbs.edu/item/is-growth-good>

13   Michael Hammer, "Reengineering Work: Don't Automate, Obliterate", Harvard Business Review, July 1990

14   Source: <https://www.forbes.com/sites/forbestechcouncil/2018/03/13/why-digital-transformations-fail-closing-the-900-billion-hole-in-enterprise-strategy/#5e7f9e3b7b8b>

15   Source: <https://techblog.comsoc.org/2019/08/29/delloro-worldwide-telecom-equipment-market-increases-after-3-years-of-decline-volte-up-16-y-y/>

16   Behnam Tabrizi and Michael Terrell, The Inside-Out Effect – A Practical Guide to Transformational Leadership, Evolve Publishing, 2013>

17   "The key to growth is the introduction of higher dimensions of consciousness into our awareness", quote from Chinese philosopher Lao Tse

18   Source: <https://www.bain.com/insights/books/mastering-the-merger/?groupCode=1>

19   Brushstroke inspired by the Zen Buddhist Enso symbol of togetherness

20   Source: <https://civicscience.com/1-5th-of-american-consumers-have-made-a-purchase-based-on-an-influencer/>

21   Source: <https://www.fastcompany.com/90406340/this-home-goods-startup-wants-to-be-an-eco-friendlier-proctor-gamble>

22   Source: <https://techcrunch.com/2019/04/22/blueland-launches-with-a-suite-of-eco-friendly-cleaning-supplies-designed-to-reduce-plastic-waste/>

23   https://hbr.org/2011/03/managing-yourself-zoom-in-zoom-out

24   https://www2.deloitte.com/content/dam/insights/us/articles/4615_Zoom-out-zoom-in/DI_Zoom-out-zoom-in.pdf

25   Source: <https://www.mulesoft.com/resources/api/what-is-rest-api-design>

26   Source: <https://www.raisepartner.com/api-revolution-risk-management/>

27   Source: <https://www.fastcompany.com/40525452/how-patagonia-grows-every-time-it-amplifies-its-social-missi>

28   Source: <https://en.wikipedia.org/wiki/Rose_Marcario>

29   Source: <https://www.ellenmacarthurfoundation.org>

30   Source: <http://wisdomofcrowds.blogspot.com/2009/12/vox-populi-sir-francis-galton.html; Emile Servan-Schreiber, Super Collectif. Fayard. 2018->

31   Source: <https://store.hbr.org/product/talent-wins-the-new-playbook-for-putting-people-first/10003>

32   Joel Kurtzman, *Common Purpose: How Great Leaders Get Organizations to Achieve the Extraordinary.* 2010. Jossey-Bass, a Wiley imprint.

33   Source: <https://hbr.org/1997/03/the-living-company

34   The Energy Project and Harvard Business Review study https://theenergyproject.com/why-you-hate-work-2/

35   PwC Study, https://www.forbes.com/sites/caterinabulgarella/2018/09/21/purpose-driven-companies-evolve-faster-than-others/#1f5c4bc755bc

36   Edelman 2012 'Good Purpose Study', https://www.disruptordaily.com/purpose-driven-marketing/

37   EY Beacon Institute 1996-2011 Purpose Study

38   Research by Millward Brown and Jim Stengel https://www.businesswire.com/news/home/20120117005066/en/Millward-Brown-Partnership-Jim-Stengel-Reveals-50

39   Kantar Purpose 2020 Study https://www.forbes.com/sites/afdhelaziz/2019/11/11/the-power-of-Purpose-kantar-Purpose-2020-study-shows-how-Purposeful-brands-grow-twice-as-fast-as-their-competition/#7589d2084236

40   Rethinking Prestige Branding by W. Schaefer & JP Kuehlwein https://www.amazon.com/Rethinking-Prestige-Branding-Secrets-Ueber-Brands/dp/0749470038

41   Patagonia is worth 1 billion USD https://www.inc.com/lindsay-blakely/patagonia-2018-company-of-the-year-nominee.html

42   Burson Marsteller Power of Purpose study http://powerofpurpose.burson-marsteller.com/wp-content/uploads/2015/04/BM_IMD_REPORT-How-Authentic-is-your-Corporate-Purpose.pdf

Few to all. All to all.

43   Johnson, Caitlin. "Cutting Through Advertising Clutter." CBS News. CBS Interactive, 17 Sept. 2006. <http://www.cbsnews.com/news/cutting-through-advertising-clutter/> accessed 6 October 2017

44   Matsumoto, David. The Cambridge Dictionary of Psychology. Cambridge: Cambridge University Press, 2009

45   Source: <https://en.wikipedia.org/wiki/Second_Life>

46   Source: ≤https://fortniteinsider.com/how-many-people-play-fortnite-concurrent-and-registered-2019-player-count/>

47   "How Many Babies Are Born Each Day?" The World Counts. <http://www.theworldcounts.com/stories/How-Many-Babies-Are-Born-Each-Day>.

48   Source: Statista, <https://www.statista.com/statistics/263401/global-apple-iphone-sales-since-3rd-quarter-2007/>

49   Source: Statista, <https://www.statista.com/statistics/216459/global-market-share-of-apple-iphone/>

50   Charles, Gemma, et al. "Brands Must Guard against 'Wikileak' Moment in Digital Age, Says Pernod Ricard CMO." *Campaign Brands Hub*. <http://www.campaignlive.co.uk/article/brands-guard- against-wikileak-moment-digital-age-says-pernod-ricard-cmo/1287257?src_ site=marketingmagazine>

51   Barton, Simon. "The Power of Purpose: How Purpose-Driven Strategy Creates More Value Than Growth *Articles | Strategy | Innovation Enterprise*. 01 Sept. 2016. <https://

channels. theinnovationenterprise.com/articles/the-power-of-purpose-how-purpose-driven-strategy- creates-more-value-than-growth>.

52   Fight Club is a 1999 cult film based on the 1996 novel of the same name by Chuck Palahniuk and serves as metaphor representing a generational shift in how we consume, perceive and use media and the effects on our personality.

53   Westenberg, Anthony. "Can We Unravel the Supply Chain?" Thestar.com. 29 Feb. 2016. <https://www.thestar.com/business/2016/02/29/can-we-unravel-the-supply-chain.html>

54   Hall, Allan. "Take Charge of Your Brand Reputation Management." SWire.com. 16 Sept. 2016. <http://www.cmswire.com/customer-experience/take-charge-of-your-brand- reputation-management/>

55   Kapferer, Jean-Noel and Bastien, Vincent (2009), The Luxury Strategy, London: Kogan Page, 2012

56   Cespedes, Frank V. and Bove, Tiffani "What Salespeople Need to Know About the New B2B Landscape." HBR.org. 02 Feb. 2016. <https://hbr.org/2015/08/what-salespeople-need-to-know-about-the-new-b2b- landscape?utm_source=Socialflow&utm_medium=Tweet&utm_campaign=Socialflow>

57   Court, David, Elzinga, Dave, Mulder, Susie and Vetnik, Ole Jorgen. "The Consumer Decision Journey." McKinsey & Company. June 2009. <http://www.mckinsey.com/insights/marketing_sales/ the_consumer_decision_journey>

58   http://interbrand.com/best-brands/best-global-brands/2016/sector-overviews/the-luxury- reset-rethinking-the-growth-strategy/

Purpose Perspectives

59   "The Naked Brand (2013)." IMDB. <http://www.imdb.com/title/tt2262281/>

60   "A Chronology of How the World's Largest and Most Profitable Automaker Drove into a PR Disaster," <http://www.motortrend.com/news/toyota-recall-crisis/>

61   Hotten, Russell. "Volkswagen: The Scandal Explained." BBC News. 10 Dec. 2015. <http://www.bbc.com/news/business-34324772>

62   "Purpose & Performance Audit and Diagnostic Tool." Issuu. 1 June 2010. <http://issuu.com/burson-marsteller-emea/docs/ppdiagnostictool?e=1598851%2F3341632>

63   White, Steven. "The Top 175 Global Economic Entities, 2011." 11 Aug. 2012. <http://dstevenwhite.com/2012/08/11/the-top-175-global-economic-entities-2011/>

64   Strauss, Mark. "Ten Inventions Inspired by Science Fiction." Smithsonian.com. 15 Mar. 2012. <http://www.smithsonianmag.com/science-nature/ten-inventions-inspired-by-science-fiction- 128080674/?no-ist>

65   The world in 2045, according to the Pentagon, World Economic Forum 2017

66   "Here." Salterbaxter / Sustainability, Purpose and Creative Communications. <http://www.salterbaxter.com/>

67   Harvard Business Review, The Consolidation Curve <https://hbr.org/2002/12/the-consolidation-curve>

68   Source: <https://fortune.com/2016/11/28/bmw-venture-capital/>

69   The dynamics of long-term growth, <https://www.sciencedirect.com/science/article/pii/0040162575900256>

70   Yamaguchi, Yuhgo. "Better Healing from Better Hospital Design." Harvard Business Review. 08 May 2017. <https://hbr.org/2015/10/better-healing-from-better-hospital-design>

71   Craig, Nick, and Scott A. Snook. "From Purpose to Impact." Harvard Business Review. 18 Aug. 2014. <https://hbr.org/2014/05/from-purpose-to-impact>.

72   O'Callaghan, Tiffany. "Sense of Fulfillment Linked to Lower Alzheimer's Risk." Time. 01 Mar. 2010. <http://healthland.time.com/2010/03/01/sense-of-fulfillment-linked-to-lower- alzheimers-risk/>

73   Mount Sinai Medical Center. "Have a sense of purpose in life? It may protect your heart." ScienceDaily, 6 March 2015. <www.sciencedaily.com/releases/2015/03/150306132538.htm>

74   Will Storr, New York Times, https://www.nytimes.com/2018/08/24/opinion/the-metamorphosis-of-the-western-soul.html

75   http://www.campaignlive.co.uk/article/natwest-hit-asa-ban-customer-charter- ad/1046592

76   Source: https://about.google/

77   Schultz., E.J. "How This Man Made Dos Equis a Most Interesting Marketing Story." Ad Age. 05 Mar. 2012. <http://adage.com/article/behind-the-work/story-dos-equis-interesting- man-world/233112/>.

78   Bhatnaturally. "Case Study Series: Dos Equis – a Triumph for Creative." Bhatnaturally. 26 May 2014. <http://www.bhatnaturally.com/dos-equis-campaign-case-study-a-triumph-for-creative/>

79   Gallup, Inc. "A Company's Purpose Has to Be a Lot More Than Words." Gallup.com. 28 July 2015. <http://www.gallup.com/businessjournal/184376/company-purpose-lot-words.aspx>

80   Adams, Susan. "Inside Hermès: Luxury's Secret Empire." Forbes. 10 Sept. 2015. <http://www.forbes.com/sites/susanadams/2014/08/20/inside-hermes-luxury-secret-empire/>

81   https://www.cnbc.com/2015/07/29/jane-birkin-requests-hermes-to-remove-name-off-iconic-birkin-bag.html

82   "World Economic Forum. The Rise of Digital Currencies. Read" – World Economic Forum. <https://www.facebook.com/worldeconomicforum/videos/10154516985311479/>.

83   Battrick, Ray. "LVMH Develops Blockchain Luxury Goods Authentication." Business Blockchain HQ, 3 Apr. 2019, <businessblockchainhq.com/business-blockchain-news/lvmh-blockchain-for-luxury-goods-authentication/>

84 Holman, Trevor, and Trevor Holman Trevor Holman. "Lamborghini to Implement Blockchain in Supply Chain Operations via Salesforce." CryptoNewsZ, 20 Nov. 2019, <www.cryptonewsz.com/lamborghini-to-implement-blockchain-in-supply-chain-operations-via-salesforce/52679/amp/>

85 "Airbnb introduces the Bélo: the story of a symbol of belonging." – YouTube <https://www.youtube.com/watch?v=nMITXMrrVQU>

86 Kang, Cecilia, and Davenport, Christian "SpaceX Founder Files with Government to Provide Internet Service from Space." The Washington Post. 09 June 2015. <http://www.washingtonpost.com/business/economy/ spacex-founder-files-with-government-to-provide-internet-service-from-space/2015/06/09/ db8d8d02-0eb7-11e5-a0dc-2b6f404ff5cf_story.html>

87 "Internet Users." Number of Internet Users (2019) – Internet Live Stats. < https://www.internetworldstats.com/stats.htm>

88 World Economic Forum 2016, Accenture: <https://www.weforum.org/agenda/2016/01/digital- disruption-has-only-just-begun>

89 15 Most Memorable Companies That Vanished. NBCNews.com. 26 Jan. 2011. <http:// www.nbcnews.com/id/41027460/ns/business-us_business/t/most-memorable-companies- vanished/#.VfCxc7QxE3E>

90 Sisodia, Rajendra, Wolfe, David B., and Sheth, Jagdish N. Firms of Endearment: The Pursuit of Purpose and Profit. New Jersey Pearson Education, 2007

On Purpose

91 Radley Yeldar. 2015. RY Fit For Purpose Index 2015. <https://ry.com/media/1160/ry-fit-for-purpose-2015-index.pdf.>

92 Harvard Business Review. 2019. The Business Case for Purpose. <https://www.ey.com/Publication/vwLUAssets/ey-the-business-case-for-purpose/$FILE/ey-the-business-case-for-purpose.pdf.>

93 Sinek, S, 2010, How great leaders inspire action. https://www.ted.com/talks/simon_sinek_how_great_leaders_inspire_action/up-next?language=en>

94 Edelman. 2017. Earned Brand 2017. <https://www.edelman.com/research/earned-brand-2017>

95 Harvard Business Review. 2019. The Business Case for Purpose. <https://www.ey.com/Publication/vwLUAssets/ey-the-business-case-for-Purpose/$FILE/ey-the-business-case-for-purpose.pdf.>]

96 Ipsos Connect. 2017. When Trust Falls Down.< https://www.ipsos.com/sites/default/files/2017-06/Ipsos_Connect_When_Trust_Falls_Down.pdf. >

97 Ipsos Connect. 2017. When Trust Falls Down. <https://www.ipsos.com/sites/default/files/2017-06/Ipsos_Connect_When_Trust_Falls_Down.pdf.>

98 Cone. 2015. 2015 Cone Communications/Ebiquity Global CSR Study. <http://www.conecomm.com/research-blog/2015-cone-communications-ebiquity-global-csr-study#download-research.>

99 Bains, Gurnek. Meaning Inc.: The Blueprint for Business Success in the 21st Century. London: Profile, 2006.

100 "To Go from "Good to Great, Be Endearing." *Good* for Profit. <http:// causecapitalism. com/firms-of-endearment/>

101 Güngören, Ahmet. "Reklamcı Ve Şaman." Kitapyurdu.com, <www.kitapyurdu.com/ kitap/ reklamci-ve-saman/24225.html.>

102 Baer, Drake. "A Couples Therapist Reveals the Most Important Quality to Look for in a Partner." Business Insider. 03 Mar. 2016. <http://www.businessinsider.com/the-most-important-quality-to-look-for-in-a-partner-2016-3>

103 Steiner, Susie. "Top Five Regrets of the Dying." Guardian. 01 Feb. 2012. <http://www. theguardian.com/lifeandstyle/2012/feb/01/top-five-regrets-of-the-dying>

104 Gallup, Inc. "How Many Teens See Purpose for Life?" Gallup.com. 06 Apr. 2004. <http://www.gallup.com/poll/11215/how-many-teens-see-purpose-life.aspx>.

105 Ro, Sam. "How The Global Wealthy Are Doing Better Than Everyone Else In One Chart." Business Insider. 05 Apr. 2014. <http://www.businessinsider.com/global-luxury-index-stock-returns-2014-4>

106 "The Global Personal Luxury Goods Market Holds Steady At €249 Billion Amid Geopolitical Uncertainty." www.bain.com. <http://www.bain.com/about/press/press-releases/the_global_ personal_luxury_goods_market_holds_steady_at_249_billion_ amid_geopolitical_uncertainty.aspx>

107 "Communication Director." Communicating Luxury, Communicating Leadership | Communication Director. <http://www.communication-director.com/issues/ communicating-luxury-communicating-leadership#.Vg0WoROqqko>.

108 Robins, Rebecca. "The Luxury Reset: Rethinking the Growth Strategy." Harper's Bazaar. 05 Oct. 2016. <http://www.harpersbazaar.co.uk/fashion/fashion-news/news/a38183/ best-global-brands-luxury- sector-growth-strategy/>

109 Kim, W. Chan, and Mauborgne, Renee. Blue Ocean Strategy, Harvard: Harvard Business Review, 2005.

110 Adapted quote from the 1989 movie Field of Dreams, symbolizing the nature of product-oriented companies producing without taking the customer into the equation.

111 "Harley-Davidson Project Rushmore, Built by All of us, for All of Us" <https://www. youtube. com/watch?v=wR0hJ39YX0Q>

112 2006-2013, Developed by Markus Kramer during his time at Harley-Davidson and Aston Martin Lagonda Ltd.

113 "Rolls Royce and the Spirit of Ecstasy" <https://www.youtube.com/ watch?v=BSgtdjdyCn4>

114 Kramer, Markus, 2017, <http://markuskramer.net/changing-nature-luxury-customers/>

115 Ipsos Affluent Survey <http://www.ipsos-na.com/news-polls/pressrelease.aspx?id=6993>

116 Edelman Good Purpose Survey 2012

117 <http://www.airbus.com/presscentre/pressreleases/press-release-detail/detail/airbus-provides-insights-into-billionaire-buying-habits/>

118 <http://www.luxurydaily.com/wp-content/uploads/2015/04/07.Ipsos_.Steve-Kraus.pdf>

119 Global Impact Investing Network, <https://thegiin.org/impact-investing/need-to-know/>

120 "Warren Buffett's Dirty Secret? Own Great Companies." ValueWalk, 20 Feb. 2018, www.valuewalk.com/2018/02/nation-the-dirty-secret-behind-warren-buffetts-billions/.

121 Source: <https://www.prweek.com/article/1523418/investor-response-crises-led-reputation-numbers>

122 Daniel Roth, Editor in Chief LinkedIn <https://www.linkedin.com/pulse/linkedin-top-companies-2018-where-us-wants-work-now-daniel-roth/>

123 The Social Responsibility of Business is to Increase its Profits, Milton Friedman, The New York Times Magazine, September 13, 1970.

124 Source: <https://www.forbes.com/sites/peterhorst/2018/01/16/blackrock-ceo-tells-companies-to-contribute-to-society-heres-where-to-start/#24968144971d>

125 2018 Global Sustainable Investment Review, Global Sustainable Investment Alliance

126 Neuromarketing – Understanding the 'Buy Buttons' in Your Customer's Brain. Patrick Renvoisé, Christophe Morin. Thomas Nelson, 2007.

127 Asset Management in Europe, 9th Edition, Facts and figures, May 2017, EFAMA, European Fund and Asset Management Association. Worldwide Regulated Open-ended Fund Assets and Flows, June 2017.

128 Winters, Riley. "John Dee: Scholar, Astrologer, and Occult Practitioner That Captivated the Royal Court of 16th Century England." Ancient Origins, <www.ancient-origins.net/history-famous-people/john-dee-scholar-astrology-and-occult-practitioner-captivated-royal-court-020412>

129 Winters, Riley. "John Dee: Scholar, Astrologer, and Occult Practitioner That Captivated the Royal Court of 16th Century England." Ancient Origins, Ancient Origins, 6 Oct. 2018, www.ancient-origins.net/history-famous-people/john-dee-scholar-astrology-and-occult-practitioner-captivated-royal-court-020412.

130 Source: <https://hbr.org/1994/03/managing-for-organizational-integrity>

131 Source: <https://www.theatlantic.com/science/archive/2017/09/cooperation-networks/538842/?utm_source=atltw>

132 Bain&Co. economic leaders' graph https://twitter.com/BainAlerts/status/785924433949130752

133 "Global Personal Luxury Goods Market 2017-2021, <www.businesswire.com/news/home/20170310005256/en/Global-Personal-Luxury-Goods-Market-2017-2021-LOreal.>

134 https://hbr.org/2016/06/ma-the-one-thing-you-need-to-get-right

GPS Guiding Purpose Strategy

135 Ray, Carolyn. "Aligning Brand, Purpose, and Culture – Views." Interbrand. <http://interbrand.com/views/grow-on-purpose -aligning-brand-purpose-and-culture/>

136 Credits go to Alex Osterwalder <https://strategyzer.com/canvas/business-model-canvas>

137 Stein, L. "Live Your Legend: Urges Harley-Davidson in New Global Campaign" <http://adage.com/article/agency -news/harley-davidson-aims-energize-brand-campaign/303141/>

138 Source: <http://www.adglitz.com/blog/2009/07/coca-cola-slogans-history-coke-punchlines-over-the-years>

139 Source: <http://www.investopedia.com/ask/answers/042315/what-apples-current-mission- statement-and-how-does-it-differ-steve-jobs-original-ideals.asp>

140 Pinker, Steven. The Sense of Style the Thinking Person's Guide to Writing in the 21st Century. London: Penguin, 2015.

141 Kondo, Marie. Life-changing Magic: A Journal: Spark Joy Every Day. Berkeley: Ten Speed, 2016.

142 "Survey Finds Employees Less Loyal Than Five Years Ago." 01 June 2015. <http://www.amanet.org/news/10606.aspx>

143 "Employee Loyalty Is a Rare Commodity." CGMA. 13 Feb. 2015. <http://www.cgma.org/magazine/news/pages/201511807.aspx?TestCookiesEnabled=redirect>

144 Imperative and LinkedIn Study of on the role of Purpose in the workforce <https://cdn.imperative.com/media/public/Global_Purpose_Index_2016.pdf>

145 Vaccaro, Adam. "How a Sense of Purpose Boosts Engagement." Inc.com. 18 Apr. 2014. <http://www.inc.com/adam-vaccaro/purpose-employee-engagement.html>

146 Freud, Sigmund, et al. Introductory Lectures on Psychoanalysis. Penguin, 1991.

147 Kahneman, Daniel. Thinking, Fast and Slow. Farrar, Straus and Giroux, 2015.

148 Morgan, Gareth. "What Does the Data Tell Marketers to Do during the Coronavirus Crisis?" Liberty Digital Marketing, 23 Mar. 2020, www.libertymarketing.co.uk/blog/what-does-the-data-tell-marketers-to-do-during-the-coronavirus-crisis/.

149 Ritson, Mark. "Mark Ritson: The Best Marketers Will Be Upping, Not Cutting, Their Budgets." Marketing Week, 9 Apr. 2020, www.marketingweek.com/mark-ritson-marketing-spend-recession-coronavirus/.

150 Quelch, John, and Katherine E. Jocz. "How to Market in a Downturn." Harvard Business Review, 1 Aug. 2014, hbr.org/2009/04/how-to-market-in-a-downturn-2.

Applying Purpose

151 "Millennial Survey 2017" Deloitte. 15 June 2017. <http://www2.deloitte.com/global/en/pages/about-deloitte/articles/millennialsurvey.html>

152 "What Makes Work Meaningful – Or Meaningless." MIT Sloan Management

Review. <http://sloanreview.mit.edu/article/what-makes-work-meaningful-or-meaningless/?utm_ medium=social&utm_source=twitter&utm_campaign=featjune16>.

153 Pinkhasov, Misha, and Nair, Rachna Joshi. Real Luxury: How Luxury Brands Can Create Value for the Long Term. Basingstoke: Palgrave Macmillan, 2014.

154 "Power Of Purpose." Power Of Purpose. <http://powerofpurpose.burson-marsteller.com/wp- content/uploads/2015/04/BM_IMD_REPORT-How-Authentic-is-your-Corporate-Purpose.pdf>

155 PwC Purpose Statement, <https://www.pwc.co.uk/who-we-are/corporate-sustainability/our-Purpose.html>

156 New York Times <https://www.nytimes.com/2014/06/01/opinion/sunday/why-you-hate-work.html?_r=1>

157 Jean-Paul Sartre, French Existentialist

158 Keller, Susie Cranston and Scott. "Increasing the 'meaning Quotient' of Work." McKinsey & Company. <http://www.mckinsey.com/business-functions/organization/our-insights/increasing-the- meaning-quotient-of-work>

159 Lyam Byrne, <https://currentaffairsonline.co.uk/2017/11/15/titans-of-history-lessons-from-the-entrepreneurs-who-built-britain/>

160 Bains, Gurnek. Meaning Inc.: The Blueprint for Business Success in the 21st Century. London: Profile, 2006.

161 Bitti, Mary Teresa. "Why Starbucks CEO Howard Schultz Is Looking beyond Profits to a Purpose-led Strategy." Financial Post. 05 June 2015. <http://business.financialpost.com/entrepreneur/why- starbucks-ceo-howard-schultz-is-looking-beyond-profits-to-a-purpose-led-strategy>

162 "Topic." International Institute for Sustainable Development. <http://www.iisd.org/topic/sustainable-development>

163 World Bank Twitter. 30 Oct. 2015. <https://twitter.com/WorldBank/status/660010976650113024>

Making it Happen

164 Borreli, Lizette. "Why A Goldfish Probably Has A Better Attention Span Than You." Medical Daily. 14 May 2015. <http://www.medicaldaily.com/human-attention-span-shortens-8-seconds-due-digital-technology- 3-ways-stay-focused-333474>

165 Stanfordbusiness. "Former World Bank President: Big Shift Coming." YouTube. 29 Jan. 2010. <https://www.youtube.com/watch?v=6a0zhc1y_Ns>

166 Hampden-Thompson, Gillian. "Stable Families, Not 'traditional' Ones, Key to Children's Education Success." The Conversation. 18 June 2017. <http://theconversation.com/stable- families-not-traditional-ones-key-to-childrens-education-success-36158>

167 Source: personal collection and consolidation of experiences, productivity literate, The

4-Hour Workweek by Tim Ferris, Getting Things Done by David Allen, The Power of Habit by Charles Duhigg, Zero to One by Peter Thiels, others

168 <https://www.virgin.com/richard-branson/power-purpose>

169 Please note, we use the term 'consumer' very broadly here; this can also be understood as prospects, co-workers, recruiters and any other audience of relevance.

170 Tom Peters in FastCompany <https://www.fastcompany.com/28905/brand-called-you>

Notes